The Pocket Guide to
CYCLING

John Wilcockson

Bell & Hyman

The Pocket Guide to Cycling
was designed and edited by
Holland & Clark Limited, London

Designer
Julian Holland

Editors
Philip Clark
Miranda Smith

Artwork by Hayward and Martin Limited

Photo Credit
Tim Hughes/Cyclographic

Published by Bell & Hyman
Denmark House, 37/39 Queen Elizabeth Street,
London SE1 2QB

British Library Cataloguing in Publication Data
Wilcockson, John
   The pocket guide to cycling
   1. Cycling – Great Britain
   I. Title
   796.6'0941   GV1041

ISBN 0-7135-2509-6

Phototypeset in Great Britain by
Tradespools Limited, Frome, Somerset

Printed and bound in Great Britain by
Purnell & Sons Limited, Paulton

Contents

Part 1 The Basics

At first sight, there are few sports and pastimes as straightforward as cycling. All you need is a bicycle, and you can pedal away from your own front door. And yet there are few pursuits that offer such a variety of interests – from kids having a 'burn-up' on their BMX machines to professional athletes battling for glory in the gruelling Tour de France.

In between these two extremes are people who ride their bikes to school, office and factory, the cycle tourists and the amateur racers. It is possible to commute, tour and race on the same bicycle – adapted for its specific task – but there will come a time when you will want to specialize.

The purpose of this book is to describe the many different facets of cycling and to show you how to enjoy your particular interests to the full, even if you are only a spectator. Cycling is a sport that has great traditions, but today considerable advances are being made in the technical sophistication of the bicycle itself, and cycling is gaining in popularity all the time.

What will never change is the amount of enjoyment you can obtain from cycling. In their different ways the dedicated tourists, the everyday commuters, those Tour de France professionals and the eager BMXers all thrill at the speed, the freedom and the rush of fresh air on their faces!

The bicycle

The basic shape of a bicycle has not changed in 100 years, but the quality and efficiency of the different elements is continually being improved. This modern 10-speed bike is typical of those available in the medium-price range. Its frame is made from lightweight tubing, and a wide range of gears make pedalling uphill as simple as riding on the flat – in theory.

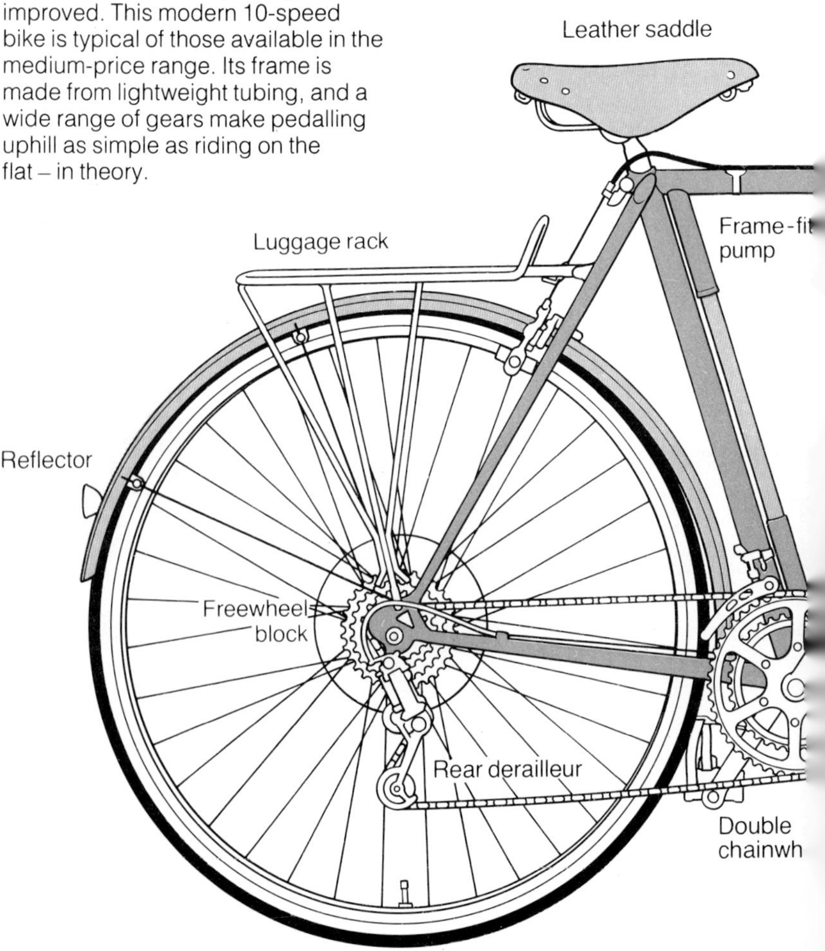

Leather saddle

Frame-fit pump

Luggage rack

Reflector

Freewheel block

Rear derailleur

Double chainwh

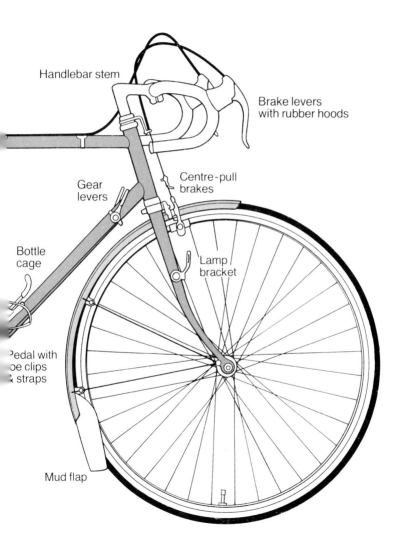

Handlebar stem

Brake levers
with rubber hoods

Gear
levers

Centre-pull
brakes

Bottle
cage

Lamp
bracket

Pedal with
toe clips
& straps

Mud flap

Glossary of Cycling Terms

Allen key Patent hexagonal shaped tool that either fits into a hexagonal recess to turn a bolt or alternatively fits over hexagonal nuts.

Ankling Method of pedalling whereby ankles are dropped below level of toes at top of pedal stroke.

Balloon tyres Wide section tyre that resembles a balloon in cross-section (also known as 'fat tyres').

Ball race Metal ring into which fit ball bearings for the turning of bottom bracket, headset or pedals.

BCF British Cycling Federation – which administers road and track racing in Great Britain.

Bib shorts Racing shorts which extend, like a pair of wide braces, over the shoulders.

Bickerton Patented folding, small-wheel bicycle made largely from aluminium alloy.

Bidon Widely used French term for a cyclist's plastic drinking-bottle.

Bikeway (or cycleway) Special path or separate section of roadway for the exclusive use of cyclists.

Block English term for the set of sprockets fitted to a freewheel for use with derailleur gears.

BMX Bicycle Moto-Cross, a sport developed in California in the eary 1970s in which small-wheeled, small-framed bicycles are raced over rough, dirt tracks.

Bonk Familiar term for fatigue caused by not eating sufficient food during a long cycle ride or race.

Boss Metal fixture brazed on bicycle frame to which are fitted items such as gear levers and drinking-bottle cages.

Bottom bracket Unit comprising metal cups, ball-bearings and the axle to which are fitted the two crank arms.

Break (or breakaway) Term in racing for one or more riders who accelerate away from the main group of cyclists.

Bunch Main group of riders in a road or track race. Also called the pack or the peloton.

Butted tubing Frame tubing that is thickened at one or both ends for added strength at the frame joints.

Cadence The rhythmic turning of the pedals at an even rate, measured in revolutions per minute (rpm).

Caliper brakes Inverted U-shaped rim brakes that operate on the principle of a pair of scissors.

Cantilever brakes Type of rim brakes used on off-road or cyclo-cross bikes (and on tandems) that give added grip and prevent clogging by mud.

Centre-pull brakes Caliper brakes that are operated by a central cable pulling up on a short section of cable looped between two brake arms.

Chainstay Oval-section frame tube that joins the bottom bracket to the rear dropout.

Chainwheel Toothed metal ring fitted to the right-hand crank on which the chain runs.

Close ratio block Freewheel block on which there is only a one-tooth jump between adjoining sprockets.

Commissaire Internationally recognized

name for the official who controls a road or track race.

Cotterless crank Crank arm that is bolted directly to the bottom bracket axle.

Cotter pin Cylindrical piece of metal with a flat, tapered edge that slots into the off-centre hole of a normal steel crank arm to fix it to the bottom bracket axle.

Crank arm (or crank) Steel or alloy arm that connects the pedal to the bottom bracket axle.

Criterium A road race held on a short circuit, normally in a town or village.

CTC Cyclists' Touring Club – national body that caters for the needs of touring cyclists, particularly their rights on the highway.

Cyclo-cross Form of racing, normally on a circuit, that includes sections of mud or tracks, and obstacles over which the bike has to be carried.

Cyclometer Mechanical or digital display unit activated by the turning wheel to register distance travelled (or sometimes speed, time and cadence).

Derailleur Front and rear gear mechanisms that shift the chain from one sprocket (or chainwheel) to the next.

Derny Small moped used for paced cycling, usually on the track.

Devil Abbreviation for a devil-take-the-hindmost or elimination race.

Directeur Sportif French term for a racing team's manager or coach.

Disc wheel Wheel on which spokes are replaced by two lenticular (or saucer-shaped) discs to improve its aerodynamics.

Domestique French term for support rider in a racing team.

Drafting American term for taking pace behind another rider.

Drop-out U-shaped metal bracket on end of front fork or rear stay into which fits the wheel hub axle.

Echelon English term for the slanting line of cyclists in a road race to combat a cross- or head-wind.

Ergometer Static exercise cycle for use in a gymnasium.

Expander bolt Bolt that screws into tapered, cylindrical block to lock handlebar stem into front forks tube.

Extension English term for stem into which the handlebars are fitted.

Fixed wheel Method of transmission in which the pedals have to be turned all the time the bike is in motion.

Fork rake The amount by which the front forks are curved from a straight line.

Freewheel Mechanism housed in metal cylinder that screws on to the rear wheel hub and allows the cyclist to stop pedalling when the bicycle is moving at speed.

General classification (or GC) Overall, positions in a stage race decided by the accumulated time of each rider on each stage.

Giro Commonly used name for the Tour of Italy, the second longest stage race in professional cycling.

Handicap Race in which the less proficient riders start a certain time or distance before the better riders.

High pressures (or pressures) English term for wired-on tyres that are pumped to a higher pressure than balloon tyres.

Honk British term for standing on the pedals, out of the saddle, to ride more easily up steep hills.

Hood Rubber covering of the brake lever.

Hooks Common name for the bottom parts of dropped handlebars.

Hub gear Variable gear mechanism contained entirely within a rear wheel hub.

Jockey Small, pulley-shaped wheel around which chain runs on a derailleur gear.

Keirin Japanese form of track racing in which riders are paced to top speed before a final (unpaced) sprint.

Kermesse Belgian town or village carnival at which a closed circuit race takes place.

Kilo Familiar name for the one-kilometre time trial event in track racing.

King of the Mountains Term applied to the best climber in a race.

Knock Another name for the bonk.

Low profile machine Racing bicycle with a top tube that slopes down to give a low, front profile which reduces drag.

Lug Metal casting into which the frame tubes fit to form joints.

Madison Term for form of two-man relay track racing that originated for six-day racing at Madison Square Gardens, New York.

Maillot jaune French term for the yellow jersey worn by the leader of a stage race such as the Tour de France.

Motor-paced Form of track racing in which each competitor is paced by a motor cycle.

Moulton Small-wheeled bicycle that was invented by the engineer Sir Alex Moulton.

Mountain bike (or all-terrain bike) A bike developed for riding across rough terrain with fat tyres, low gears and wide, straight handlebars.

Musette Light canvas shoulder-bag that is used for carrying food during a race or long distance touring ride.

Open A race in which amateur teams are permitted to compete against professionals.

Ordinary Formal name for the 'penny-farthing' or high bicycle popular in mid-Victorian times.

Oxygen debt The phenomenon of overstretching your physical resources, and having to gasp for air.

Pace line American term for a line of cyclists who take it in turn to set the pace.

Panniers Luggage bags fitted on metal racks either side of the front or rear wheels.

Positron Patented derailleur system in which the lever clicks into correct position for each change of gear.

Prime Racing term (pronounced 'preem') for an intermediate cash prize, usually at the end of a lap or the top of a hill.

Plus ones Tight-fitting breeches that end just below the knee and are worn with long stockings.

Pursuit Track race in which a rider (or team) starts from a different point to the opponent, and each pursues the other for a set distance or until one is caught by the other.

Quick release Mechanism used on hubs to allow wheel release without using a tool.

Roadster Traditional, heavy bicycle with balloon tyres and straight handlebars.

Rollers A set of three cylinders joined by a metal frame on which a bicycle can be ridden without forward movement. Often called a home trainer.

RTTC Road Time Trials Council – administers time-trial racing in England and Wales.

Sag wagon (or broom wagon) Vehicle that follows last rider in a road race in order to transport any competitor who retires from the race.

Shoeplate Metal or plastic, slotted plate affixed to the sole of the shoe to allow the foot to be placed firmly on the pedal.

Side-pull brakes Caliper brakes that pivot on a centrally-fixed bolt with a cable attached to one of the brake arms.

Sitting in (or on) Racing term for a rider who 'sits' behind others, taking shelter from the wind, without personally making the pace.

Six-day Track race contested by two-man teams in relay fashion on six successive days.

Skinsuit All-in-one shorts and top used for track racing, shorter road races and cyclo-cross.

Soigneur A racing team's masseur or coach.

Sprints and tubs English term for lightweight wheels and tubular tyres.

Stage race Series of road races (or stages of which the winner is the rider with the lowest combined time for all the stages.

Stem The component through which the handlebars are connected to the headset. Also called handlebar extension.

Tandem Bicycle that has seats and pedals for two riders, sat one behind the other.

Ten-speed Common name for a lightweight bicycle that has derailleur gears with ten separate gear ratios.

Time trial Race in which each competitor starts (normally at one-minute intervals) and races alone over a set course with the winner being the one who takes least time. (A team time trial is the same, but with each team of usually four riders working together to achieve the shortest time.)

Toe clips (and straps) Metal or plastic clips that hold a leather strap which fixes the shoe firmly to the pedal.

Track ends Rear fork ends on a track bike from which the wheels have to be removed away from the frame, not downwards or forwards as on a normal frame.

Track nuts Dome-shaped nuts that screw on to conventional wheel-axles to tighten the wheel in the frame.

Tubular (or 'tub') High-pressure, ultra-light tyre with inner tube sewn into the outer cover, which in turn is glued on to the wheel rim.

UCI Union Cycliste Internationale – the international governing body of cycling.

Velodrome Banked, oval-shaped cycling track, normally with spectator accommodation.

Yellow jersey See **Maillot jaune**.

Types of Bicycle

Racing
Strength and lightness are the two main characteristics of a bicycle used for racing. These qualities are obtained by building the frame with double-butted tubing and fitting it with aluminium alloy components. A recent development is the use of much more streamlined wheels, cranks, gears, brakes and pedals.

Touring
A heavier gauge tubing is used for the frame, which has shallower angles than the racing bike. Lower gearing is necessary as well as racks to support the panniers, saddlebag and handlebar bag. Also a priority on a touring bike are mudguards and lighting.

Shopping
A small-wheeled bike is popular with shoppers because there is more room to place a heavy load on the rear luggage-rack. In consequence, the design necessitates wider, thick-treaded tyres to provide adequate support. This type of machine is mostly suited to short urban trips.

Folding
This type of small-wheeler is ideal for the cyclist who has to travel a lot by rail or road. It can be folded quickly, placed in a bag and assembled again at your destination. The best kind of folding bicycle is made from lightweight frame tubing and has high quality, alloy components and multiple gearing.

BMX

Designed for racing on dirt tracks or for performing stunts, the BMX bike has a small, one-size frame which gives wide clearances to the small, knobbly wheels. Other features are the single, low gear, the steel cranks, high-rise handlebars and the low saddle position. *It is not meant for use on the public highway.*

Off-the-road

There are various names for this hybrid machine, including 'mountain bike' and 'all-terrain bicycle'. Its principal features are a shallow-angled frame, straight, wide handle-bars, a wide range of gears, fat tyres, cantilever brakes and finger-tip controls. *It can be used on the public highway.*

Tandem

It does not take a genius to calculate that two people weigh more than one; so sturdier wheels and tyres, and stronger brakes are essential features of a tandem. To avoid 'whip', various methods of frame construction are used to distribute the weight evenly. Lower gearing is also necessary for efficient climbing.

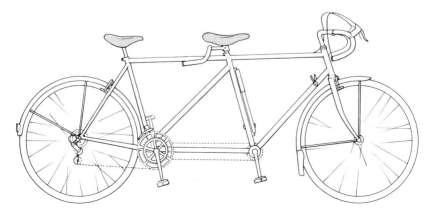

Choosing a Bike

Whatever type of cycling you intend to do, it pays to buy the best bike you can within your price range. This is particularly true if you are going to use it for racing, long-distance touring or everyday commuting, when efficiency and reliability are essential.

From the earlier pages you will know what type of bicycle is most suited to your purposes, but how do you distinguish between a 'good' and a 'bad' bicycle? After all, they all look very much the same in a particular range, don't they?

Unless you know exactly what you want in the way of frame and all the various accessories, and you can afford to pay for something made-to-measure, then you will certainly have to settle for some form of compromise. The first priority – always – is that the bike should be the right size for you.

It is amazing how many people ride a bike that is much too large (with the saddle practically sitting on the top tube) or too small (with their knees banging up against the handlebars as they pedal). And yet it is a simple task to choose a bicycle that is just about the right size (see 'Correct Riding Position', page 20).

Once you have made certain what size frame you need, the next task is to make a list of the different parts that you need. For instance, it is a waste of money to buy a bike with, say, 18 gears (three chainwheels and six rear sprockets) if you are going to ride it in a completely flat area. You *could* ride a bike with 18 gears on flat roads, but you would be better off with perhaps a five-speed, or even a single-geared machine.

Once you have made a general specification of your 'ideal' bike, the next task is to see what is available on the market. Take a look at current magazines, books and catalogues. Make a visit to one or two local bicycle shops for a more detailed study of machines that are in your price range and 'fit the bill'.

Do not be afraid to ask for advice from the shopkeeper or from friends who are experienced cyclists. To get exactly what you want, it is possible that you will have to look for a second-hand bike – either study the 'For sale' columns of the local newspaper or a specialist publication.

Many shops, of course, also deal in used bikes; they may also sell off machines which have been used in a bike-hire business. If so, you are likely to get a better guarantee of reliability than from a private seller.

Ideally, if you are buying a new bicycle, you should go to the best local cycle shop – one where you will have probably seen many club cyclists on a Saturday. You can be sure that a reputable dealer will not sell a bike that is the wrong size or has not been thoroughly checked over and correctly adjusted.

If you have to buy by mail-order then make sure that you get the assistance of someone knowledgeable to help set up the bike. It is essential to have correctly adjusted brakes and gears.

The bicycle is the most expensive item you need to acquire; make sure that you buy the right one.

The frame

The traditional diamond-shaped frame is an assembly of 14 different-sized tubes, and it is the quality of the tubing that distinguishes a good one. Ordinary steel tubing produces a frame that weighs almost twice that made with butted alloy tubes. Look for a small label on the seat tube with brand names like Reynolds 531 (or the slightly heavier 501), Columbus or Vitus; these are all drawn from high strength alloys. A second-hand frame should be checked for alignment – the wheels should be perfectly in line with each other – and for possible crash damage.

Saddles

Contrary to popular belief, a sprung saddle is not the most comfortable, particularly on longer trips. The pedal action makes you bounce from side to side, and a firm seat is essential to an efficient output of energy.

This factor is most important in the context of a race so the racing saddle is normally of treated leather on a light steel frame, or of stiff moulded plastic covered with a thin foam layer and a suede-type top.

Many tourists prefer to use a racing saddle, but the more comfortable alternatives have a slightly wider base or thicker foam padding on the plastic. It is important to take good care of the saddle, using the recommended proofing cream for leather and a brush for suede.

A BMX saddle is rarely sat upon, and then only for balance or when performing stunts, so a simple plastic seat is sufficient. But make sure you keep it clean.

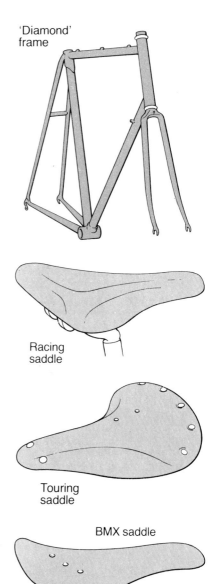

'Diamond' frame

Racing saddle

Touring saddle

BMX saddle

Handlebars

So-called dropped handlebars are suitable for most types of cycling. They are liked by tourist and racing cyclist alike because they allow you to adopt three distinct positions.

The most common one is to grip the rubber brake lever hoods – comfortable on the flat and ideal for climbing out of the saddle. For extra pull when in the saddle going uphill, you can grip the centre part of the handlebars. While riding into a wind, or racing to cut down the air resistance, you can hold the lower parts of the handlebars – the 'hooks'.

In contrast, straight handlebars offer only one position for the hands, and as a consequence, backache is a potential problem on longer trips.

Brakes

It is a legal requirement in most countries for a bicycle to be fitted with two fully operational brakes, one of which can be a fixed wheel. The lightest and most efficient are caliper brakes, which are operated by a cable being pulled forward when the brake lever is used.

It is essential that the cable moves smoothly within its housing and that the brake mechanisms are adjusted (see 'Maintenance' page 91). On a used bike replace the old brake blocks.

If maintained correctly, both side-pull and centre-pull brakes provide good service, although cheaper models tend to pull over to one side. Alternatives are hub brakes or back-pedalling ('coaster') brakes.

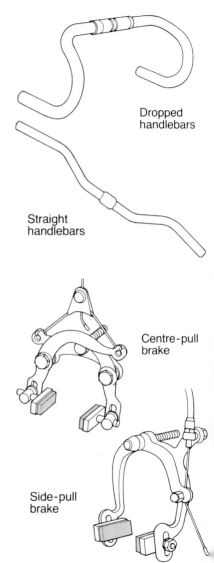

Dropped handlebars

Straight handlebars

Centre-pull brake

Side-pull brake

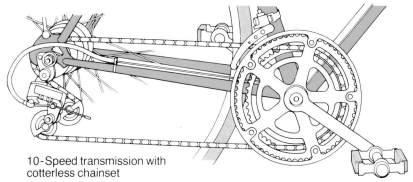

10-Speed transmission with cotterless chainset

Chainset and gears

The production of derailleur gears and cotterless chainsets is one of the most competitive sectors of the cycle industry. Consequently, the standards are generally high, and only the racing expert should seek out the most expensive items.

On a used bike, look out for worn teeth on chainwheels and sprockets, and for a stretched chain. It may be necessary to replace all three items.

As with brakes, the gear cables should run smoothly and the gear mechanisms should be kept adjusted.

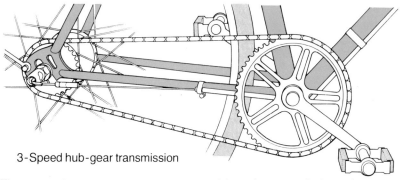

3-Speed hub-gear transmission

Three-speed

A three-speed hub gear does not offer as much flexibility as a derailleur, and it is heavier – but it is popular for everyday cycling because of its efficiency and undemanding maintenance. Again,

cable maintenance is the major deterrent to smooth operation. Replace a frayed cable immediately, and always keep the adjustment nut tightened. As with a cotterless chainset, the chainwheel and sprocket should be kept free of grit.

Correct Riding Position

It is sometimes said that anybody can ride a bike. All you have to do is sit on the saddle, push down on the pedals and – as long as you can balance – you're away. But it takes time to learn to ride a bike *correctly*.

It is all too common to see a bicycle being ridden in too high a gear by a cyclist whose heels are hard against the backs of the pedals. They are making hard work of what should be a fluid, efficient type of motion.

The key to a good cycling style is a frame of the correct size. When you buy a bike, a rough guide is to deduct 10–12 ins (25–30 cms) from your inside leg measurement to give your ideal frame size – the distance between the bottom bracket axle and the top of the seat tube. For most people, a frame of between 21 and 23 ins (53–58 cms) will suffice.

Finding your correct riding position is now a case of adjusting the height and position of the saddle and handlebars, as shown in the illustrations on page 21.

For normal riding, the saddle can be slightly lower than for racing, while the handlebars can be raised to the same height as the saddle. These adjustments allow you to have a more upright posture for better visibility, and to reach the ground more easily with one foot on stopping at traffic lights.

To make the most of the 'ideal' position, the balls of the feet should be on the pedals. This is the reason why serious cyclists use shoe plates, toe-clips and toe-straps. Do not be afraid of these locking your feet to the pedals.

Sideview of rider
The aim of a good riding position is to give your body plenty of room, while maintaining as streamlined a profile as possible. At the same time, the body should be steady – not rocking from side to side – and the legs should be moved smoothly.

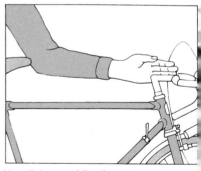

Handlebar-saddle distance
A rule of thumb is that the distance between the tip of the saddle and the top part of the handlebars should be the length of your forearm (from the back of elbow to finger-tips). In practice, the distance can be slightly longer than this.

Saddle height

With the bicycle supported somehow
– perhaps by a friend – alternately sit
on and adjust the height of the saddle
until you feel a slight stretching at the
back of the knee when your heel is on
the pedal. The saddle can also be
adjusted laterally, so the forward
movement should be set before the
height is determined. However, there
is a second check: with the pedals
and cranks in a horizontal position,
the centre of your knee-joint should
be vertically above the pedal axle. If a
further adjustment of the saddle is
required, then a second check is also
needed for its height, and of the
distance between the saddle and the
handlebars.

Adjusting saddles

When adjusting the height of the
saddle – as here with a spanner on a
retaining bolt, or with an inset Allen
key-bolt – always ensure that it
remains in line with bike's top tube.
When twisting the saddle upwards,
pin the rear wheel between your
knees to keep the bike steady.

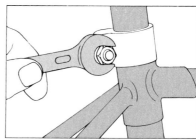

Adjusting the handlebars

The handlebars should always be at
the same height as the saddle, or
about 2 ins (5 cms) lower. To adjust
the height of the stem, you have to
loosen the top nut, and then take a
small block of wood and bang the
handlebars down as shown.

   The stem bolt screws into a wedge-
shaped cylinder which grips the
inside of the fork tube when fully
tightened. the banging down loosens
this cylinder.

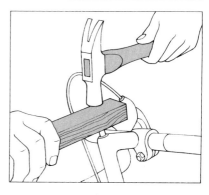

Road Sense and Safety

Whatever type of cycling you choose to do, much of your time will be taken up with riding on the open highway, probably in towns or cities, where keen road sense is as important as good style. Most road accidents take place on urban streets, and that is why an early appreciation of the apparent dangers is important.

In Britain, the cycling proficiency test of the Royal Society for the Prevention of Accidents is a good starting-point for children to learn how to ride correctly – but the theory has to be put into practice. Too many so-called cyclists disregard rules of the road, and ride through red lights or go the wrong direction along one-way streets. If you respect the rules, other road-users are more likely to respect you.

A bicycle is a road vehicle, not a toy, and as a cyclist you should behave as part of the normal traffic. You are not a pedestrian on wheels.

You should always know what other vehicles are around you so that you are prepared when you need to make turns. And keep a special look-out for pedestrians who can step out unexpectedly. To sum up: always act with confidence and responsibility.

SETTING OFF

Position your bike near the edge of the road, with your left foot on the kerb and your right foot ready to push *down* for the first pedal stroke. Make sure that you are in a low gear, and then look firmly behind to check that the road is clear before starting.

Having made sure that it is safe to set off, accelerate gently to your normal riding speed before changing up into a higher gear (if you have gears). It is best to ride up to 3 ft (1 m) from the kerb to avoid grit and drain-covers, and to give yourself room to manoeuvre.

Turning left

Above: You do not have traffic indicators on a bicycle, so all changes of direction should be clearly signalled. To turn left, it is usually best to make two signals; firstly, well before the junction, before you brake or slow down; and secondly after you have braked, to confirm your intentions to following vehicles and pedestrians crossing a side street.

Overtaking

Right: Whether you are about to overtake a parked car or a slower moving vehicle – perhaps another cyclist – always signal your intention *after* checking that it is safe to move out into the centre of the road. And do not wait until the last second. It is a part of essential road sense to think ahead, observing traffic at all times.

Turning right into major roads

When you are approaching a T-junction, always make sure you know which direction you want to take. If in an unfamiliar area, stop about 100 yards before the junction, and consult your map or closely observe the road signs.

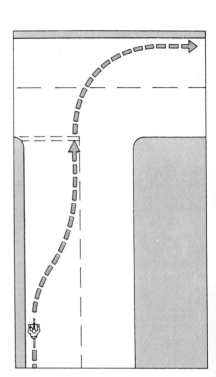

If you want to make a right turn, make clear your intentions well before you reach the junction. If you turn and see that fast traffic is about to pass you, slow down until it is safe to begin moving into the centre of the road – and always accompany this movement with a clear and positive right-turn signal.

If there is a right-turn lane, use it. If not, move gradually to the centre of the road, keeping a look-out behind and in front as you make the move. Do not leave space for vehicles to go outside you, pinching you between two lines of waiting vehicles. Remember, you are part of the traffic and cars also have to stop before turning into the major road.

Before you stop, make sure that you have changed down into a lower gear so that you are ready to accelerate away from the junction. Stop with your left foot on the ground and with your right foot ready to push down on the pedal.

Before setting off again, look left and right, taking particular note of vehicles that may be turning right into the same street or road as yourself. Again, give your right-turn signal and, *only* when it is clear, push off and ride smoothly away in a wide curve to the opposite side of the main road. Make a final check to your left as you reach the centre of the road.

Turning right from major roads

This is potentially the most hazardous turn that a cyclist has to make – particularly after dark. Because of this a confident approach is a must.

As with the previous turn, make sure which road you wish to take well before the junction. If other vehicles are also turning right you should move with them – they will be moving at about the same speed as you, slowing down and probably stopping. There is added protection in moving at the same time as cars.

Once again, change down a gear or two before reaching the junction in case you have to stop. Turn your head two or three times before you start your manoeuvre because most of the fast-moving traffic will be going straight on. You will have to wait until there is a big enough gap in the traffic flow for you to cross to the right side of the road before you make your right-turn signal.

When you have signalled, move decisively so that any continuing fast traffic can pass you on your left. Make your signal before you start the turn, and then put out your arm a second time as you reach the centre of the road.

If you are forced to stop by oncoming traffic or a red light, be ready for a quick getaway – left foot on road, right foot at top of the pedal stroke – and keep your hand out until the second you accelerate into the side street or road.

Finally, watch out for any pedestrians who may be crossing the side street or road and give following vehicles plenty of space to overtake on the road you are now riding along.

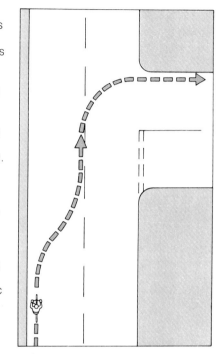

Roundabouts

Turning right
Making a right turn at a roundabout is similar to making a right turn from a major road (see previous page), but you have the added ingredient of giving way to traffic which is already on the roundabout. If the roundabout is free, do not stop, but signal clearly that you are turning right. And accelerate away quickly to make the turn, being wary of traffic which is going straight on.

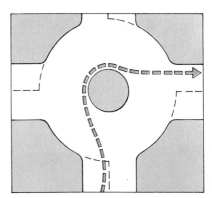

Turning left
This is a much simpler move than making a right turn, but you must still show caution. Make your left-turn signal and wait until there is a clear gap in the flow of traffic on the roundabout. Be particularly wary of traffic that is moving quickly across the roundabout and taking the same road as you – they are inclined to cut corners. Always keep an eye on vehicles approaching you from behind.

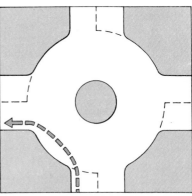

Straight on
Observe the usual rules of changing down a gear so that you are ready to accelerate through the junction – as shown in the drawing. Pay particular attention to vehicles behind you or at your side that may be turning left. They do not always signal, and you could easily be cut up. If it is a large roundabout, do not forget to make a left-turn signal before you leave the roundabout.

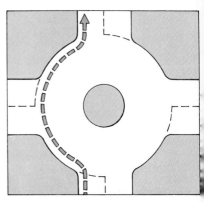

Coping with Hazards

However proficient you are in making the various moves shown here, you will still have to allow for the unexpected. A pot-hole may cause you to swerve, a car may turn across in front of you without the driver looking, or a vehicle may stop suddenly. You have to be prepared.

Coping with unexpected hazards is an essential part of road sense. You can take precautions to deal with hazards like the weather – wearing the right clothing is one important rule.

In windy weather, beware of sudden gusts blowing you off-line. You can prepare to combat these by observing the direction of the wind and where it is likely to blow from the side. If the rain (or hail, or snow) is so heavy that you cannot see clearly, take shelter until conditions become safer.

A second type of hazard is the one that is static: a pot-hole, a badly placed grating, a bump in the road, a steep hill or an oil-slick. You can take evasive action by keeping your eyes open and reacting before it is too late.

Treat obstacles like bumps, pot-holes and gratings the same as you would a parked car: signal that you are going to move out to give other traffic plenty of warning. In the case of parked cars, also beware of an off-side door being opened in front of you.

If you are forced to ride over a pot-hole or bump, slow down and lift yourself out of the saddle to take pressure off the rear tyre – this could mean that you avoid a puncture or even a buckled wheel.

On any slippery surface such as an oil slick, ice or in the wet, do not make any jerky movements. Use a higher gear to keep acceleration to a minimum; do not suddenly jam on the brakes; and try to steer in a straight line.

Similar advice applies for descending hills, with the additional tip of applying the brakes in cadence fashion to slow from a high speed. This means alternately putting on and releasing both of the brakes.

The third area of hazard is other road-users, who may make a mistake or drive without caution. Be prepared for anything.

At traffic lights, for example, do not squeeze between the kerb and a large vehicle. They will not see you and could turn left across your line. Squeezing between two lines of traffic holds similar dangers.

On left turns, a vehicle could cut across in front of you – be prepared to turn left with it.

In heavy traffic, particularly on narrower roads, always keep well in to the edge and, if in a group, travel single-file.

It always pays to be patient when you are cycling. Other road vehicles are bigger than bicycles and it is invariably you who will get the rough end of any collision.

You should also read the Highway Code which, although far from perfect, contains some sensible advice for cyclists – particularly that about keeping a safe distance behind other traffic, not carrying unbalanced loads and fitting front and rear lights and a reflector. And always check the lights are working.

Part 2 Types of Cycling

Few sports offer as many opportunities as cycling. From the fit to the not so fit, from the under-fives to the over-80s – there is something for everyone.

Once you have mastered the basic skills – balance, good posture, gear-changing, road sense – you are ready to progress to one of the various types of cycling. There are several ways open to you when taking up cycling as a sport. Most towns and cities in the British Isles have either a touring, racing or BMX club. You can get advice on who to contact from a local library or bike-shop, or one of the national bodies that control the sport (see Appendix: Organizations and publications).

Most cycling clubs cater for all types of cyclist and they give you an ideal opportunity of trying out different pursuits – touring, road racing, track racing, time trials or cyclo-cross. Most BMX racing is organized by specialist clubs, while mountain biking is a relatively recent introduction, with few clubs.

It is important that you join one of the national bodies that offer free third party insurance and legal aid (the British Cycling Federation or the Cyclists' Touring Club in Great Britain). This is necessary in case of accident. Another good investment is a sturdy padlock, and insurance against theft for your bike (this may be an addition to the family's house-

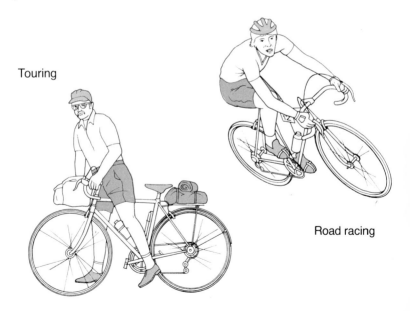

Touring

Road racing

hold insurance). Theft of bicycles is one of the more common crimes all over the world.

If you are going to take up racing then joining a club is essential, but a tourist can quite easily enjoy his interest alone. Indeed, one of the attractions of touring is the freedom it offers. There are few holidays that can equal the pleasure of a week's cycling tour; and few as inexpensive if you stay at youth hostels or bed-and-breakfast establishments.

Many riders progress from touring to racing after acquiring greater skills at covering long distances and climbing hills on their touring bikes. A semi-competitive sector of the sport – known as randonneur or Audax riding – has become popular in recent years.

It is generally found that the mid-teens are the best time to start a racing career, although some well-known professionals have not taken up the sport until they were well into their 20s.

At the other end of the age-scale, there are comprehensive programmes of racing for the over-40s, both in road racing and time trials. And it is not unknown for time trialists to continue racing into their 80s.

Yes, cycling is a sport that is popular with all age groups and both sexes. If you would like to see which type of cycling appeals most to you – read on!

Mountain bike riding

BMX racing

Touring

A bicycle is a passport to a new life, a passport to adventure. On your first ride of any distance you will discover places that you never knew existed. Drifting down a country lane, or along a river bank, a bicycle can make you aware of the joys of nature – even within a few miles of a town.

As you become more ambitious, and more adventurous, you will find that cycle touring offers all the ingredients of a perfect outdoor pursuit: fresh air, good exercise, low costs and an infinite variety of places to visit. A bike is suitable for a round-the-world expedition and also for a brief morning ride before work. The choice is yours.

It is one of touring's chief attractions that you can set off from your own doorstep.

With the changes in season and weather, the same stretch of road can seem a very different place in summer and winter. And a bicycle is 'sympathetic' with its surroundings: you travel at the pace of the country-side, you can smell the aroma of newly-mown hay and the scent of spring flowers, and – most important – the bicycle is silent.

You will be able to observe the birds and the animals of the *real* countryside without disturbing them – that's something that a motor-pow-ered traveller will never be able to achieve. That's cycle touring. Try it!

Below: Touring in the wide open spaces of North America, these well-equipped cyclists ride the hard shoulder.

The touring bike

A woman's frame is shown here as an
example, although most cycle tourists
prefer the extra strength of a normal
'diamond' frame. Buy the strongest
frame you can afford.

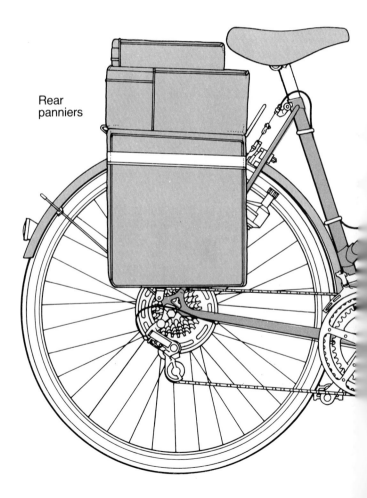

Rear
panniers

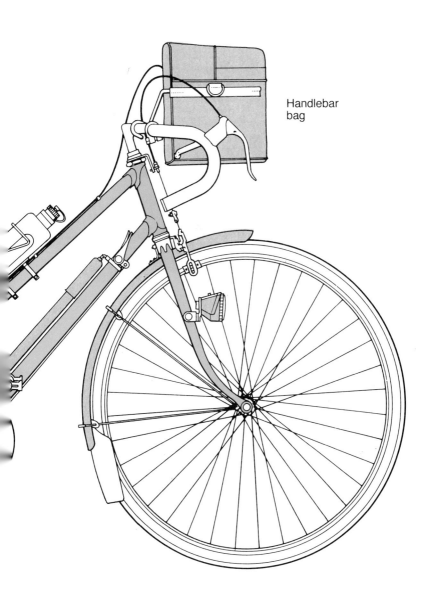

Handlebar
bag

Touring – Clothing

Summer

In theory, you can ride a bike in any type of clothing you like. But just as you would not play football in your best suit, there is no reason to wear tight-fitting jeans for cycling – especially today when the quality and choice of cycle wear has never been better.

In summer, you obviously do not need as much added warmth as in winter, but it is just as important to wear the most suitable clothing.

Starting from the feet, a pair of thin white ankle-socks (not thick ones) should be worn with proper cycling shoes – not soft-soled trainers, which do not transfer your leg-power very efficiently and are likely to cause cramp. It is also desirable to have shoeplates which prevent your feet from sliding about on the pedals.

The stretch fabric of custom-made cycling shorts gives a comfortable ride, and they have a double-skin seat to give greater wear than a normal pair of athletic shorts. And remember that white shorts will quickly become stained, especially if you have a leather or black-topped saddle.

A simple T-shirt is suitable for most summer weather, but you will find that two layers are usually preferable, especially to combat the rush of air when going downhill. A short-sleeved cycling jersey has pockets at the rear, in which you can comfortably place enough food and a map, perhaps some tools as well, (including a spare inner-tube) for a good day's trip. When touring in mountains, a track suit will keep you warm if the weather turns cold.

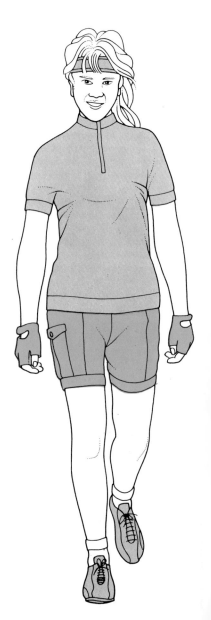

Winter

Gloves and headwear are common to both summer and winter touring. In warmer winter weather (and the whole of summer), open-backed 'track mitts' are ideal for protecting hands in the event of a fall, and for absorbing some of the vibration from the handlebars. Of course, cold weather necessitates proper gloves – possibly even two pairs in freezing conditions, a thin pair underneath and thick, woollen gloves on top.

Some tourists feel that the added protection of a hard-shell helmet is necessary in all seasons and in all traffic conditions. Otherwise, a light racing-type cotton cap is ideal for sunny weather (the peak can be pulled down to prevent glare) and a woollen ski-type hat is perfect for cold weather.

In addition to a T-shirt and cycling jersey, a tourist needs a thick track-suit top or woollen sweater for most winter riding. In cold conditions, a long-sleeved undervest is perfect when used in combination with tights or long-legged underpants.

There should be no tightness at the waist, so cycling breeches (or plus-ones) should be supported by braces, not a belt. Long stockings, as shown here, should be wool; or use two layers of thinner legwear.

As for the feet your summer cycling shoes can be used if they do not have ventilation holes, otherwise buy a pair of lined shoes or some of the plastic-coated overshoes that are·popular among racing cyclists.

A scarf can also be useful in winter weather, combined with a balaclava helmet when it is icy.

How to Plan a Tour

Whether you plan to be away for a few hours or a few weeks, a cycle tour can be far more pleasurable if you spend a little time with a map before setting out. There are certain things that you should take with you, as well. And the sooner you learn which the better.

Discovering different routes, even in your own area, can take days, months, perhaps years. So it is of great assistance if you can find out about good cycling roads as soon as possible. Joining a local cycling club or the DA (District Association) of the CTC is one way of finding out. Otherwise, there may be cycle route mapbooks that cover your area. These will help you until you can add your own discoveries.

One of the first things you need is a detailed map of your home area. If you live in the UK, the best choice is the 1:50,000 scale map produced by the Ordnance Survey – there are about 200 such maps covering the whole country.

These maps show every important landmark, including churches, post offices, youth hostels, windmills, rivers and lakes, and will soon help you familiarize yourself with the local countryside. If you are going further afield, maybe for a long day ride or a weekend, the 1:100,000 scale of the Bartholemew's series will give you sufficient guidance.

Seek out the quieter routes, maybe the B-roads or unclassified roads, even if it means adding a few miles to a journey. You will find that most motorists, buses and big lorries stick to the more direct routes, the A-roads or motorways.

Do not try to be overambitious on your first daytrips. You may ride your bike to the station every day, perhaps two miles each way, but you will find that your legs will start to ache and your seat will be tender if you attempt, say, a 100-mile ride on your first Sunday out.

You will discover that you will become extremely hungry on a long trip, so it is as well to plan a route that passes through several villages. Take some food and drink with you as well, to replace all the burnt-up calories.

You must also think about your bike. Before setting off on a trip, preferably the night before, check over the machine. Test the brakes and gears; pump up the tyres and look for any flints or glass wedged in the tread; put a spot of oil on the chain if necessary; and give the whole bike a quick once-over with a clean rag.

Obviously, for weekends away or for longer journeys you will need a comprehensive range of tools so that you can replace broken spokes, frayed cables or a defective freewheel (see the section on maintenance, pages 78–85).

The map opposite shows a well-planned route for a daytrip, starting and finishing at the East Anglian town of Saffron Walden. By taking a longer total route, it is possible to shorten the ride very easily if you need to turn back. The cut-through at Finchingfield is a good example. Plan to make a stop for lunch around halfway; and a tea-stop as well for longer rides.

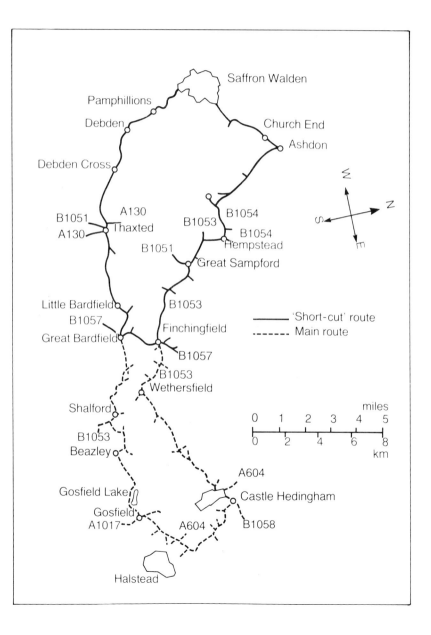

Most experienced tourists use a small saddle-bag or handlebar bag for daytrips, so they know that they always have the essential tools and spares should they need them. The bare minimum is perhaps a small screwdriver, an adjustable spanner (or small, boxed set of spanners) and tyre-levers (with puncture repair kit or spare inner tube) if you are using high pressures. Do not forget your pump, padlock and water-bottle. And lights if you expect to return late in the day.

One consideration when planning any tour is of course the weather. Listen to the forecast each day and act accordingly. If a strong west wind is blowing, for instance, plan a route that brings you back with the wind behind you. If a cold evening is forecast, take a tracksuit top and some gloves, just in case. And avoid the hills if bad weather is predicted for higher ground.

A last useful tip is to take some extra money for emergencies. If it is a daytrip, for example, you may need coins for telephone calls and enough money for a train trip home.

INTERPRETING MAPS

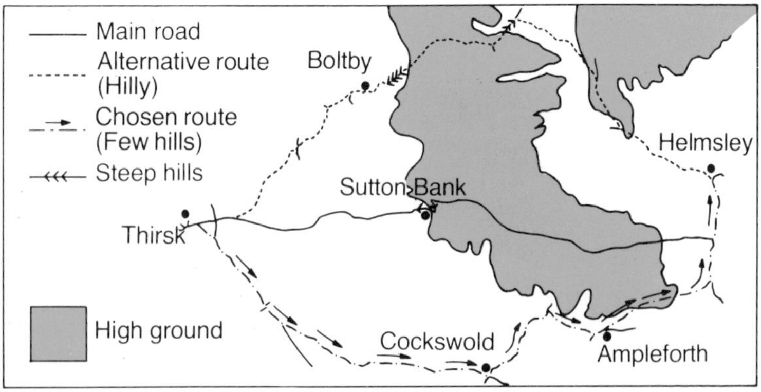

- —— Main road
- - - - - Alternative route (Hilly)
- —→ Chosen route (Few hills)
- ‹‹‹— Steep hills

High ground

Boltby
Helmsley
Sutton Bank
Thirsk
Cockswold
Ampleforth

The most direct route between two points is not always the quickest or the best one by bicycle. As in this example, the shortest way is over a hill – as indicated by the contours, which are lines joining points of equal height. Where the contours are close together, the gradient is steep. The alternative routes are longer, but do not include any steep climbs.

The best way to learn map reading is to take a map with you wherever you go and compare what you can see with what appears on the map. With practice, it is surprising how many cross-country routes you can take without using main roads – and you can avoid the hills, if you want to.

Good map reading can help the cycle tourist seek out the most beautiful stretches of terrain.

Planning a Touring Holiday

Once you have made several day-trips, the next stage in your cycle-touring education is a weekend away. This will open new terrain to you and make you look at the sport in a different and exciting way.

This will require more planning, and you will need to buy another map. Your two days should take in some of the notable sights of the new area.

A weekend tour is ideal preparation for a full touring holiday. This can be a traditional 'tour' that starts and finishes at the same point with separate overnight halts; a point-to-point ride; or a fixed centre tour.

If it is a first big tour, do not be overambitious. It is better to plan for, say, a 50-mile-a-day schedule rather than finding that 80 miles is leaving you struggling every day. And, on

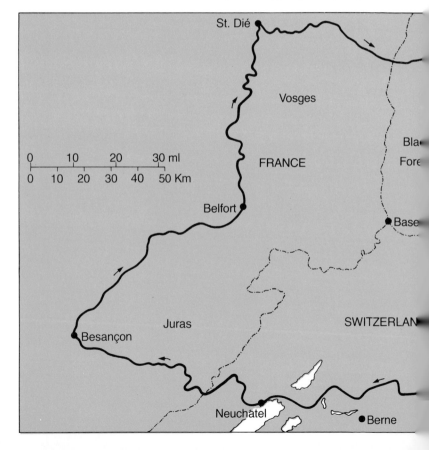

the shorter schedule, you can always get in some extra miles with a short ride in the evening.

There are many books which will give you detailed ideas of where to tour (see the **Bibliography**, page 92), while group holidays with the CTC or other organizations are also a possibility. If you are planning it alone, study as many travel books as you can before choosing.

This week-long tour passes through three European countries, France, West Germany and Switzerland, and traverses three mountain ranges, the Vosges, the Black Forest and the Juras. Using the suggested overnight halts, an average of 100 kms (62 miles) a day would be maintained. Besançon, Strasbourg and Basle have good train links with either Paris or the Channel ports.

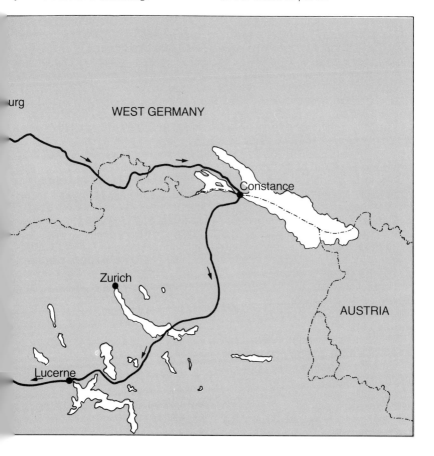

Touring – Riding in a Group

Many cyclists prefer to ride alone or with just one companion, but it can be even greater fun travelling with a group – either other members of a club or in a family unit.

Club runs represent one of the best traditions of the sport and, besides the camaraderie, you will find that group riding makes distances seem much shorter. The reason, of course, is that air resistance is the main force acting against a cyclist – alone you are fighting it for the whole of your day's ride, in a group of 20 you endure it for perhaps only ten per cent of the time.

It takes skill to ride effectively in a group and there needs to be a steady change in the 'wind-breakers' at the front. The best method is to adopt a rotational formation in which the group forms two lines, one moving forwards and the other returning to the back of the group.

At normal touring speeds – 15 to 20 mph (24 to 32 kph) – each rider stays at the front for about two minutes, maybe longer if the conversation is good! It is usual for a run 'leader' to choose the day's route and this rider's instructions should always be heeded, whether it is to 'turn left', to 'stop' for a puncture repair or to 'slow' for one of the members who is having trouble keeping up.

Sometimes, the group does split up out of choice, and because of this it is as well to have the planned lunch and tea halts known to everyone. A pub, café or tearoom are all likely stopping-places – or perhaps you can have a picnic during the summer months.

Touring in a family group is not quite the same because there are bound to be a wider range of skills than among the members of a club. This is why a tandem is a popular choice for many husband-wife combinations.

Young children can be carried on baby seats for perhaps the first four years of their lives, while they can become fairly independent from the age of seven onwards. It is also possible to obtain an adaptor for children so they can ride on the back seat of a tandem.

Riding in a group is one of the best methods of *really* learning how to ride a bike. You can observe more experienced cyclists and ask them about things you do not understand. And they will probably help you perfect your riding style and teach you some of the 'tricks' used for emergency repairs.

On a touring holiday, it is best to restrict numbers to about six people, unless you have done extensive planning and reserved accommodation for the whole tour. Also, you will find that punctures and mechanical problems constantly plague a large group. Keeping the group compact gives everyone more time to enjoy the holiday.

Right: These British club riders naturally form two neat lines to cycle efficiently against the wind.

Racing

There are few more impressive sports than bicycle racing. Anyone who experiences for the first time the Tour de France, for example, cannot fail to be enthralled by the race's spectacle. A snaking, multi-hued line of 180 machine-mounted athletes racing through incomparable mountain scenery is an unforgettable sight.

Life in the pack of riders can be harsh. They have to climb the highest Alpine roads, fight oxygen-debt in merciless time trials and pit themselves against each other over dust-filled, cobbled farm-tracks. Racing in burning heat or icy rain, it's all the same to a Tour de France professional.

At the other extreme, a skinny-legged 14-year-old could be starting a cycling career in a club 10-mile time trial on a deserted backroad in the English countryside. The path to competing in a Tour de France would be a long and often lonely one, possibly reaching its destination via open time trials, track league meetings, junior road races and amateur internationals.

Few cyclists reach the summit of their sport, and few really have the ambition to do so. But whatever level you reach you can have great fun. You will learn a lot about yourself, both physically and mentally. Cycle racing is not all about brute strength: fitness is essential, but finesse is also needed in all aspects of the sport.

The Racing Bike

Compared to the mass-produced ten-speed bike, the racing bike is built to much more exact specifications. The frame is of lighter, stronger tubing and made-to-measure for the rider. The lighter, sprint wheels are fitted with one-piece tubular tyres. The saddle is slightly higher and the handlebars lower to give the best aerodynamic position. Gearing is higher and closer spaced. And toe-clips and toe-straps are essential.

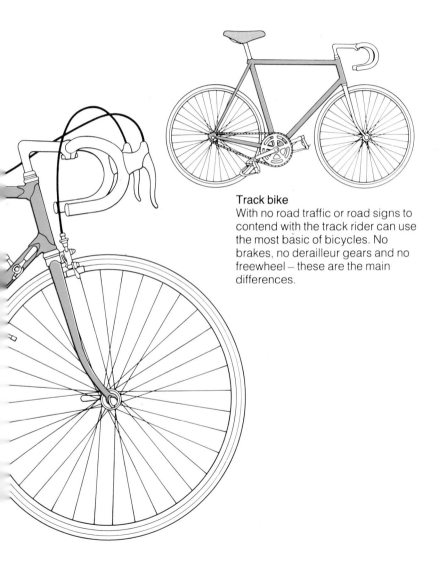

Track bike
With no road traffic or road signs to contend with the track rider can use the most basic of bicycles. No brakes, no derailleur gears and no freewheel – these are the main differences.

Racing Clothing

Just as a racing bike is more stream-lined than a general purpose bi-cycle, so the racing cyclist's clothing is equally devoid of frills. Tight-fitting, but stretchable fabrics are used to create an attractive, highly practical outfit. Items vary for the different types of racing and for changing weather conditions, but the following summary describes the basic needs.

For shorter time trials, for track races and short-distance road races (up to 90 minutes), the main item of clothing is the skinsuit. This has shorts and jersey combined, with a zip from the neck to the navel. Long-sleeved versions can be bought for colder weather.

The skinsuit is worn with an undervest, perhaps a cotton T-shirt, to absorb sweat and give two layers of clothing to prevent heavy grazing in the event of a crash. The shorts have a chamois leather insert in the seat, which is sometimes coated with lanolin cream for an even smoother ride.

For all types of racing, white ankle-socks and leather-palmed open-backed track mitts are stan-dard – except in cold weather when woollen (or even rubber) gloves and perhaps black tights are also worn for added protection.

A modern adaptation of the skin-suit for road racing is the bib short, which extends over the shoulders to obviate the need for braces. A normal racing jersey is worn over the top of bib shorts. This has pock-ets at the back to hold food and perhaps a drinking bottle.

In cold weather, it is normal to wear two racing jerseys, at least one of which should have long sleeves. And in wet weather, it is wise to use a racing cape – this is a jacket fastened with Velcro, and perhaps made from a material such as Gore-tex that prevents overheating.

The best quality racing shoes are narrow, with perforated leather uppers (to keep the feet cool) and thick, rigid soles that have integral shoeplates. These plates have to be adjusted and locked tight to give a firm grip of the shoes on the pedals – a slot engages with the back-plate of the pedal (or with one of the patented pedal locking mechanisms that do not require toe-clips and toe-straps).

For cold or wet weather, plastic, fitted overshoes can be used to protect your ankles as well as your feet (and valuable shoes). For cyclo-cross, the shoes also have studs or even spikes to give a grip on slip-pery, running sections of the course.

For all track and road racing in Great Britain and Ireland, a crash-hat (or helmet) is obligatory. The traditional type is made from padded strips of leather (perhaps plastic-coated) and a leather chin-strap. Gaining in popularity are more substantial helmets, some hard-shelled, which offer more pro-tection in the case of a heavy fall on the head, but provide less venti-lation.

Headbands are often worn to absorb sweat in hot weather, or rain. And white, cotton cycling caps are also popular, the peak offering some form of protection from bright sun-shine or heavy rain.

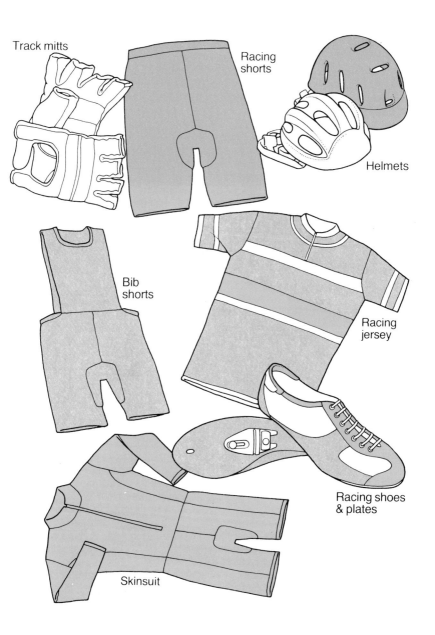

Track mitts

Racing shorts

Helmets

Bib shorts

Racing jersey

Racing shoes & plates

Skinsuit

Racing – Getting Started

After you have taken part in a few club runs, maybe an organized tour or one of the increasingly popular *randonneur* trials (normally a 50-, 100- or 200-kilometre route to be ridden within a certain time), then you may start thinking about actual racing.

If you are not already in a club, then join one; you will then get all the advice you need to begin a racing career. For a club time trial or a schools race, you could use your normal ten-speed bike, less the mudguards, lights and racks. But the time will soon come when you have to invest in racing wheels and a proper racing bike.

At one or two tracks and permanent circuits, it is possible to ride bikes that have been supplied by local authorities or education boards for children to learn a new sport. Otherwise, it is usually possible to borrow and later buy a second-hand bike through a club.

To do well at racing, it will be essential to do some form of training, preferably in the company of more experienced riders. Youngsters in particular should not overdo training – there is plenty of time for that when you become a senior.

To compete in races open to all-comers, you have to fill in a standard entry form. There are different forms for each type of racing, and each has different entry conditions.

For instance, you have to enter road races more than three weeks in advance as fields are restricted to 60 riders on open roads. Selection for each race is usually done on merit. If you are not picked, you may be put on a list of reserves (substitutes) who may replace those who do not arrive in time for the start of the race.

Circuit races have different entry deadlines, while time trials have to be entered two weeks in advance. Most cyclo-cross events accept entries on the line.

As the illustration shows, there are a number of requirements. For road, circuit and track races, you will need a racing licence, obtained through your club. You will also have to keep a detailed record of all your achievements so that you can fill in details such as 'best three road race performances' and your 'best times over each of the standard time trial distances'.

You will probably find that it is easier to get accepted for races at the end of the summer, when entries traditionally tail off, so this would be a good time to try your first races. Also, you will reap the benefit of a summer's cycling in your legs, and the weather is likely to be kinder than in early spring.

It is unusual for anyone to start winning races as soon as they take up the sport, so never worry if your early performances are not spectacular. Listen to advice, learn by your mistakes and try to adapt your training to improve performance.

As the months pass, and you race more regularly, you will find that everything begins to become more natural.

Right: You need to keep detailed records of your racing to fill in entry forms.

APPENDIX 2
AMATEUR ENTRY FORM FOR TRACK AND ROLLER EVENTS UNDER BRITISH CYCLING FEDERATION RULES

The Organiser must enter the following details of the meeting in the space below: Name of Promoting Club, Sponsor, Title of Meeting, Date and Time, Closing Date, Venue and event details, Entry Fee, Organiser's Name and Address, Prize Values.

To the Organiser:

Please enter me for ....

on .... I enclose P.O. value.....................................

I declare I am an Amateur/under B.C.F. Rules and that the information on this form is complete and correct. I understand and agree that I participate in this race entirely at my own risk, that I must rely on my own ability in dealing with all hazards, and that I must ride in a manner which is safe for myself and all others. I agree that no liability whatever shall attach to the promotor, promoting club, race sponsor, the British Cycling Federation or any race official or member of the British Cycling Federation or member of the promoting club in respect of any injury, loss or damage suffered by me in or by reason of the race, however caused.

Signature of entrant .... Date...........................

USE BLOCK LETTERS

SURNAME ....

FORENAMES ....

Address ....

....

Club ....

No.. Mark ....
(Handicapper to complete)

Date of Birth ....

Colours ....

Category............................... Licence No. ....

LAST EVENT RIDDEN (at each of Distances now entered)

EVENT	Date	Distance	Scratch Man	H/cap or Sc'th	Mark	Placing Heat	Placing Final	Winner Name	Mark
1.									
2.									
3.									

LAST THREE PERFORMANCES in Handicap events

1.									
2.									
3.									

LAST HANDICAP EVENT IN WHICH A PRIZE WAS WON

1.									

ENTRIES WITHOUT CORRECT FEE OR DETAILS WILL NOT BE ACCEPTED
These forms available from B.C.F., 70 Brompton Road, London, SW3 1EN, @ £1.50 per 100 (includes postage).

APPENDIX I
AMATEUR ENTRY FORM FOR ROAD AND CIRCUIT RACES UNDER BRITISH CYCLING FEDERATION RULES

The Organiser must enter the following details of the event in the space below: Name of Promoting Club/Sponsor, Title of Event, Date and Time, Closing Date, Categories, Course Details and Distance, Event H.Q., Organiser's Name and Address, Prize Values, and Entry Fee.
To the Organiser:

Please enter me for _____ I enclose entry fee of

I understand and agree that I participate in this race entirely at my own risk, that I must rely on my own ability in dealing with all hazards, and that I must ride in a manner which is safe for myself and all others. I am aware that when riding on a public highway the function of the marshals is only to indicate direction and that I must decide whether the movement is safe, I agree that no liability whatever shall attach to the promotor, promoting club, race sponsor, the British Cycling Federation or any race official or member of the British Cycling Federation or member of the promoting club in respect of any injury, loss or damage suffered by me in or by reason of the race however caused.

THREE BEST EVER PERFORMANCES		
Date	Event	Placing

PERFORMANCE IN LAST FOUR EVENTS RIDDEN		
Date	Event	Placing

Points gained last season	Points gained this season

(Block Capitals Please)

SURNAME ....

FORENAMES ....

ADDRESS...

....

CLUB..

DATE OF BIRTH..

CATEGORY...

LICENCE NO..

CLUB COLOURS ....

I declare that I am an Amateur under B.C.F. Rules and that the information on this form is complete and correct. I do/do not wish to be nominated as a reserve.

SIGNED ....

DATE..

ENTRIES WITHOUT CORRECT FEE OR DETAILS WILL NOT BE ACCEPTED
These forms available from B.C.F., 70 Brompton Road, London, SW3 1EN, @ £1.50 per 100 (includes postage).

Road Racing

Since 1869, when an Englishman, James Moore, won the world's first road race between the French cities of Paris and Rouen, the sport has steadily developed throughout the countries of Europe – and now throughout the world.

Unfortunately, for British cyclists, road racing ran into legal problems at the end of the last century, and while racing on the open road grew into a major sport in France, Belgium, Italy, Holland and Spain, the story was very different in England. Unpublicized, individual time trials replaced proper road racing, and instead of events like the Tour de France developing, only set-distance time trials became established.

It was not until after the Second World War that racing and bunched racing became legalized on the roads of Britain – and only then for a maximum field of 40 riders. This has since been increased to a maximum field of 60 riders.

Races are organized for school-age children, for juniors (under 19) and for three categories of senior

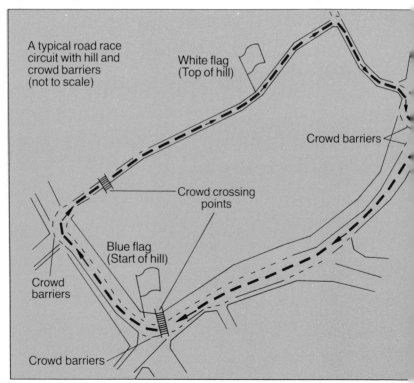

A typical road race circuit with hill and crowd barriers (not to scale)

White flag (Top of hill)

Crowd barriers

Crowd crossing points

Blue flag (Start of hill)

Crowd barriers

Crowd barriers

amateur. You need to be a first category rider before you can progress to the élite ranks of the professionals.

There are restrictions on gears and lengths of races for younger riders, with schoolchildren only racing on closed circuits over distances less than 24 miles (40 kms). Juniors race over distances up to 74 miles (120 kms), while the longest amateur races are less than 124 miles (200 kms). Circuit races (or *criteriums*) are usually of 12 to 62 miles (20 to 100 kms).

Circuits vary from less than ½ mile (800 m) to perhaps 25 miles (40 kms), with the aim being to give a good balance between hills and fast, flat sections. In Britain, a number of flags are used to indicate different features: a chequered flag for the finish, a yellow flag 200 metres from the line and a white flag for an intermediate 'prime' or sprint prize. An average road circuit avoids extremely narrow lanes and busy main roads for obvious reasons. Police permission is required before any course is approved for racing.

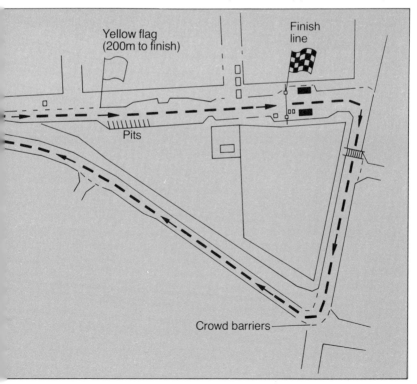

Hill Climbing

Few road race circuits are without hills, and therefore an ability to climb is one of the prime qualities of an ambitious rider. This does not mean that you need the strength to tackle ten-mile long Alpine passes, but even on short circuits you often have to climb a 300-yard stretch with a 1-in-10 (10 per cent) gradient, for example.

Even if you have the best sprint finish in the world, unless you can keep up with the stronger climbers it is of no use to you. Conversely, a rider without a good sprint invariably has to attack on a hill, as this is the only section where a decisive lead can be created by a lone rider.

The strength and the direction of the wind can also create the right environment for an attack, but it normally takes a group of riders to take advantage of this, not just one individual.

In major races, crowds always gather on the hills because they know this is where they are going to see some action – whether an attack, or the ejection from the back of weaker riders.

Unless the gradient is shallow (less than 1-in-20, 5 per cent), you will need fairly low gears to climb. You will be going much slower than on the flat, consequently air resistance is not a major factor; technique and power-to-weight ratio play far more important roles. Clearly, lightly-built riders have an advantage over heavier competitors but this natural advantage has to be developed to achieve real climbing success.

Patience is one of the main virtues of a good hill climber, especially in longer road races. If you make a big effort at the foot of the hill, the chances are that you will be going into oxygen debt before the top – you will have overstretched yourself. It is far more effective to let others burn up their energy on the first part of a climb while you wait until just before the summit to launch an attack. You can then catch everyone out when they are stretched to the limit.

To make such a break effective, it is best to attack using a bigger (higher) gear than your opponents. Obviously it takes confidence, strength and prime fitness to carry out such a plan – and that is why road racing is such a challenging sport. You are always having to take small gambles, and unless you attempt such moves you never know if they are going to be a success. Before you can reach such a state of proficiency you will make lots of mistakes – it takes patience to progress.

To improve your climbing ability, practice riding up hills without getting out of the saddle, or even riding without your hands pulling on the handlebars. This way, you will increase the strength of your back muscles while improving your actual climbing technique. And when you do stand on the pedals to attack in a race, you will really fly!

Right: Hill-climbing is one of the more difficult disciplines in the British time trial calendar.

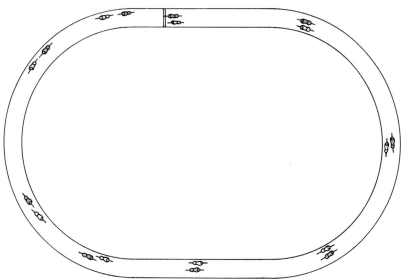

Sprinting

In modern racing, most group sprints are fought out on very high gears, unless there is a steeply uphill finish. Therefore, a good sprinter is often a rider who has worked particularly hard at weight or power training. It takes great courage to force a way to the front, and the difference between winning and losing is often down to 'throwing' the bike at the line at the vital moment.

Teamwork tactics

There are two basic moves that a team of a leader and three support riders can perform tactically. The aim is to put the leader into a winning position. If a break develops, one team rider should go with it to slow its progress. If the leader is in the break,

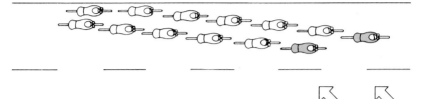

Racing in wind

Learning to ride correctly in a group is the most effective way of retaining energy for the important phases of a race, and this means doing your share of the pace-making.

You have to learn how to ride as closely as possible to the rider ahead of you: your front and his rear wheel will probably overlap slightly. In well-formed echelons, only the front riders are not protected from the wind.

the other three will slow the progress of any chase by so-called blocking tactics.

To favour a sprinter, the team ride hard at the front of a pack to prevent breakaways developing. A rider slows a break by leaving gaps that others have to close.

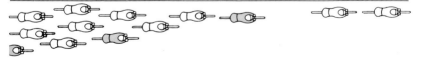

Time Trials

Time trialing – racing against the clock and not directly against an opponent – is all about technique, not tactics. Strength, fitness and ability to push oneself are all important elements in a good time trial performance, but perhaps of great significance are judgment of pace, style, gear selection and mental concentration.

The longer the race, the more important becomes the technique. This point is emphasized by the remarkable performances of veteran (over-40) riders in British time trials, many of whom produce faster times than they had in their youth, perhaps 20 years earlier. They have acquired high skills in all the different facets of time trialing and these compensate for any reduction in athletic ability.

The time trial is the traditional form of racing in the British Isles, with most events being held over the standard lengths of 10, 15, 25, 50 and 100 miles, 12 hours and 24 hours. The 25 is the most popular set distance. There are often prizes on handicap and for the fastest team. There is growing support for circuit time trials over hilly routes, as opposed to the standard main road courses, while team time trials (for two, three or four riders a team) are also contested.

A time trial special

This aerodynamically designed time trial bike has oval shaped frame tubes to reduce drag, narrow profile wheel rims and tyres, streamlined handlebars and no exposed brake cables. It extremely light in weight.

For competitors at the highest level, refinements such as these can mean the difference between winning or losing a crucial time trial. The extra expense can save vital seconds.

The bulk of the air drag is caused by the rider, therefore the use of teardrop-shaped, aerodynamic helmets is also a factor which can help save a few more seconds. Other small refinements include one-piece skinsuits, coverings to shoe laces and longer cranks (to obtain more leverage).

Few of these costly improvements are required by the ordinary competitor, who is more than happy to set a personal best performance.

In British time trials, the order of start is based on each rider's previous best performances. In a maximum field of 120 riders, the fastest riders would be given start times 10 minutes apart, with the top two usually given numbers 120 (last man to start) and 60. Riders start at one-minute intervals.

When there is a time trial in a stage race, it is normal for the overall race leader to start last, preceded by the second, third and fourth placed performers, while the rider last on overall time is the first to start.

Compared with a normal road racing position, the rider's body can be more stretched. The aim is to keep the upper body as parallel to the top tube as possible, while giving yourself enough room to breathe. This is done by slightly raising the saddle position and lowering the handlebars (or fitting deeper handlebars).

It is usually found that the most effective method of riding is to use as high a gear as possible without losing your momentum. The gear should be turned as evenly as a metronome to be fully effective. A series of accelerations will quickly tire you, whereas a steady pedalling rhythm or cadence will demand a constant output of energy.

If you reach the finish without feeling exhausted then it is clear that you have raced below your possible best – you should try riding a slightly higher gear on your next time trial.

Below: The hands as low as possible on the handlebars, the upper body parallel to the top tube, the head tucked in and the eyes concentrating on the road ahead – these all contribute to the best riding position.

Track Racing

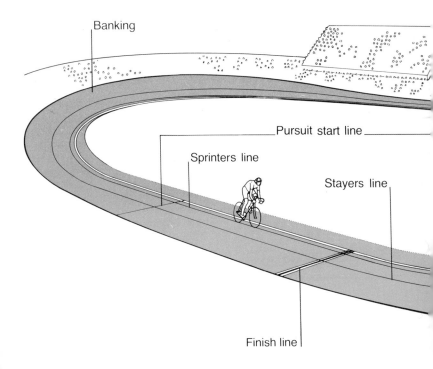

Banking

Pursuit start line

Sprinters line

Stayers line

Finish line

Compared with the often rugged and destructive nature of road racing, track racing has a glamorous, clean-cut image. From the thrill of a 10-second 40 mph sprint, to the excitement of the final hour of a six-day race, this branch of the sport is all about speed and showmanship.

There are three basic types of track rider: the thick-thighed sprinter who has the ability to produce a powerful acceleration over a short distance; the long-limbed pursuiter who can maintain a pace around 30 mph (50 km/hr) for up to six minutes; and the all-rounder who performs best in a points race that demands endurance and sprinting skill.

Velodromes – the universal name for cycling track arenas – vary enormously in size and scope. The smallest are the indoor tracks, which could be as small as ten laps to the mile. These are used for six-day racing in the winter. The largest are the old-fashioned ovals sited around football pitches which could have a circuit of up to 546 yds (500 m).

The highest quality tracks are constructed of either dense hardwood or smoothly compacted concrete. Asphalt is a popular all-

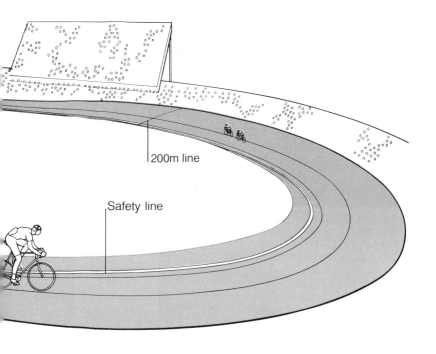

200m line

Safety line

weather surface, while shale and grass tracks also exist.

The tighter the bends on a track, the steeper the banking necessary to allow riders to race at high speeds. Experienced performers learn to make use of the bankings when making an attack.

In Britain, the usual way of beginning to track race is to participate in a local track league.

Meetings of local track leagues take place on weekday evenings through the summer, with riders scoring points in each race for their clubs. The most popular events are

Track racing is strictly controlled to make it as safe as possible. Around the inside of the track is a safety line, inside which no competitor is permitted to overtake an opponent. The sprinters line, 35 ins (90 cm) outside the safety line has a similar role in a sprint race: a rider inside the line can only be passed on his outside. A third of the way up the track is the stayers line. Also marked are a finish line at the end of the home straight, a line across the track 200 m from the finish and pursuit start lines midway along the two straights.

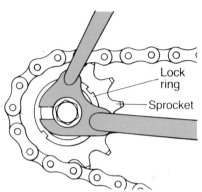

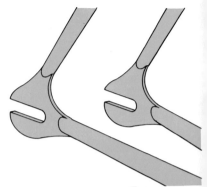

A fixed sprocket is screwed directly to the hub, giving direct transmission from the chain. To prevent the sprocket unscrewing (this is possible if a rider slows down by back-pedalling), a locking ring has to be fitted for track racing.

The safety feature of a track racing bicycle is the shape of ar fork ends. The wheel has to be removed backwards, not as on road bikes. This is to prevent a wheel pulling forward in the event of the hub not being fixed firmly in place.

the sprint, pursuit (or short time trial), points race, elimination race and Madison. Also promoted are team pursuits, motor-paced races, handicaps, keirins and scratch races. (A keirin is a sprint race between, usually, nine riders who start in a group together.)

A sprint takes place between two or three riders, the aim being to manoeuvre themselves into a winning position on entering the final (timed) 200 metres. Interval training, racing-speed repetitions and weight training are some of the methods of preparation for the sprinter.

In a pursuit, the two competitors start from opposite sides of the track, with the aim of pursuing and catching the opponent, or recording a faster time over the set distance – 3000 m for juniors and women,

4000 m for senior amateurs and 5000 m for professionals.

A normal distance for a points race is 31 miles (50 km). On an average-sized track of 364 yds (333 m) circumference, there are sprints every fifth lap through the race, with points awarded to the first four riders each time. The competitor with the highest points total wins unless any other riders have managed to break clear and gain a whole lap on the rest of the field.

A Madison is a variation on this theme, except that it is contested by teams of two riders, who relay each other at 500 m intervals.

This is the basis of six-day racing

Right: On a shallow-banked track, these riders are taking part in a team pursuit competition.

Cyclo-cross

What began as a fun thing to do in the off-season has become a fully-fledged branch of the sport with its own regional, national and world championships. Cyclo-cross has been compared to cross-country running with bikes, but it is far more sophisticated than that.

Cyclo-cross races are demanding in the extreme and this is why even the professional world champion-ship is a race of little over an hour's duration. A typical circuit would be about two miles (3 kms) around with a certain number of definite obsta-cles – steep banks where a bike has to be carried, low hurdles, perhaps even a ditch to jump. In between the obstacles are fast stretches of riding, on grass, mud, gravel or asphalt. To excel you need nerves of steel and huge reserves of energy.

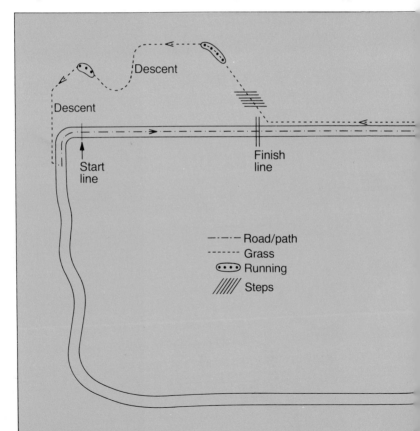

There is technical ability involved in dismounting, shouldering your bike for a run-up, setting off again on the flat and then pedalling up a track on loose gravel. The real experts make it look easy with all the different elements combining into one smooth operation. The lesser riders frequently come to a halt as they puzzle over the best thing to do at a certain obstacle.

Being confined in a small area, perhaps a parkland setting, cyclo-cross has grown into a popular spectator sport as well, even though conditions can often be cold, wet or snowy. It is probably the least hidebound sector of competitive cycling as most events can be entered on the start line. World championships for professionals, amateurs and juniors are held each year.

A Typical Course

The map shows a typical cyclo-cross circuit of about two miles (3 km) in length, of which about eight laps would be made in a race lasting one hour: in dry conditions an average speed of 15 to 20 mph (24 to 32 kph) is common. The course shown here is based on a road circuit, with the finish point halfway along a section of tarmac on which the race would start. Proceeding in an anti-clockwise direction, the riders make a sharp right off the track on to grassland, with a long descent to the foot of the course. This is followed by a short climb to a tarmac surface before looping around a lake (mud would probably be a problem here) to the first of four banks where the bikes will have to be shouldered. Following the second of these run-ups is a drop down to the edge of the finish straight for a ride across grass, before turning right to climb some steps. Two last climbs and descents precede the fast track section. In major events, pits would probably be set up at the lake and at each end of the finish straight.

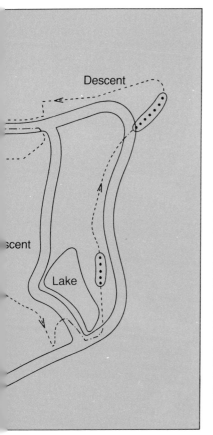

Descent

scent

Lake

A majority of competitors take part simply for the enjoyment of careering down steep banks and racing along woodland paths – even if the frequent, exhausting climbs sometimes reduce their pace to a crawl. But the also-rans receive as much encouragement as the stars in this popular pastime.

To compete at the highest levels takes extreme dedication and the best quality equipment. Ultra-light, aluminium alloy frames make the task of running much easier, while 'knobbly' treaded tyres give better grip in mud and sand.

Particular attention has to be paid to pedals and toe-clips: the rider is constantly getting off the bike and remounting, so the feet are going in and out of the pedals throughout the race. There is also a high chance of the pedals hitting obstacles around the course – tree roots, loose rocks or course marker-posts. This is the reason why most experts opt for reinforced, double toe-clips that are not going to bend or break on impact.

Riding through mud and fallen leaves can also present problems as the wheels become clogged. So a cyclo-cross frame will have extra clearance between tyres and tubes when compared to a road bike, while cantilever brakes are used for the same reason.

Even so, mud can easily cling to other working parts: the chain, free-wheel, derailleurs and chainwheels.

A cyclo-cross bike features a light alloy frame to make carrying easier; a single chainwheel, and plastic or aluminium rings, to prevent chain derailing; a handlebar gear lever; a plastic saddle and 'knobbly' tyres for a better grip.

To combat this problem, the best riders have two or three complete bikes with them at a race, and a team of helpers will hand up a spare machine to their rider and clean the muddy one before they come around on the next lap. The spare machines are also on hand in case of mechanical problems or punctures.

In world championship races and all international cyclo-crosses, areas known as pits are roped off for the machine changes to take place; and it is normal for the pits to have a bike-washing facility – hose-pipe, high-pressure spray or a convenient stream!

To avoid congestion on the often narrow paths, the field is usually limited to about 50 or 60 starters. And the start itself takes place on a wide section of paved road or across an open meadow, so that the group is stretched into a long line before it reaches the circuit itself.

It can be difficult to pass slower competitors on wooded sections or on footpaths, so there is always a fast pace set at the beginning to obtain the best positions. Unlike other mass-start forms of racing, there is little use for sophisticated tactics or pace-sharing. It is normally the riders at the front who remain there until the finish. Only when there is a fast, easy course do road racing techniques have any real significance.

In closely fought races, when two or three riders have a chance of winning, it is not always the strongest who wins. By observing his opponents' techniques at the different obstacles, he can judge the moment to attack – perhaps on the approach to a hill or a hurdle, where the riders have to dismount. Rarely is a sprint finish necessary!

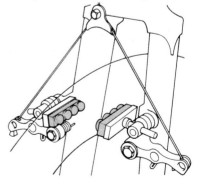

Two toe-clips are riveted together to prevent them bending or snapping when the pedal hits a rock or tree root. They also help the rider to replace his foot on the pedal after dismounting.

Cantilever brakes are essential to prevent mud and leaves clogging the wheels. Normal brakes restrict the clearance between tyre and frame tubes. The brakes shown give better performance on steep descents.

Mountain Bikes

There was no such thing as an off-road, all-terrain or mountain bike before the mid-1970s, but racing on these hybrid machines had become quite popular by the 1980s. It has become an important sector of the sport in the United States, where the mountain bike was first designed to negotiate the dirt trails and mountain tracks of California and Colorado.

It made sense to equip a bike with fat tyres and wide-ranging gears to ride on wild terrain. The first races were long trips across real mountains, but modern mountain bike contests can take many forms: uphill or downhill time trials, short-circuit races on unpaved streets, trials of skill on rocky trails, mass-start races over several laps of a hilly circuit, or the ride across the mountains.

One of the obvious features of a mountain bike is that the frame is smaller than a rider would use for a cyclo-cross or road race. There are two main reasons for this: to give a high clearance for the bottom bracket (to lessen the chance of pedals hitting rocks), and to give a low saddle height when on steep climbs (a quick-release bolt enables the saddle to be raised or lowered without dismounting).

The frame also has wide clearances for the wheels, and smaller diameter wheels are fitted. The fat tyres have a thick, knobbly tread and low air pressure to provide maximum grip on rocky uphills. As with cyclo-cross, cantilever brakes are used.

Thumb-tip gear levers enable the rider to keep hands on the handlebars at all times, with the wider, straight bars providing the maximum amount of control on sandy or stony trails.

Two, or sometimes three chainwheels are fitted to provide gears low enough to climb the steepest tracks while giving a gear large (high) enough to speed on a downhill run. A wide-ranging freewheel block is also essential.

In America, riders have to be self-sufficient in mountain bike races. No spare wheels can be used, so a competitor has to carry a pump, a spare inner tube and enough tools to carry out minor repairs.

It is normal to wear plus-ones and long stockings (even in races) because of the need at times to ride through vegetation. It is also less painful on the legs if you fall off on a rocky trail! A hard helmet is also advisable.

There is a tendency for racers at the highest level to use toe-clips and straps, but it is more usual to employ the specially produced, wide rat-trap type pedals, which have small pointed projections to give a better grip for the soles of running shoes or boots, the normal footwear.

The best performers at this form of competition are those with a background of normal cycling – they need the cardio-vascular fitness for climbing mountain trails – allied to a high degree of acquired skills. Descending steep, rock-strewn paths demands a special technique, and plenty of bravado.

A mountain bike is cumbersome to carry because of its weight (many items are bulkier than those on a road bike to give added strength),

and it takes considerable riding skill to climb steep hills while remaining in the saddle.

It is unlikely that the mountain bike will obtain the same popularity in Europe as it has done in America, Australia and South Africa, because of the lack of suitable trails. Some forms of the all-terrain bike are used by people who ride mainly in towns, where the fat tyres can be useful to counteract pot-holes and broken glass. But the wider tyres are more difficult to ride on normal roads.

This mountain bike competitor is well prepared for a long-distance race, with a pump behind the seat tube, two drinking-bottles on the down tube and a spare inner tube and tools strapped under the saddle. Note the straight handlebars with easily accessible gear and brake levers, the wide-ranging freewheel block, and the quick-release lever to adjust the seat height while on the move. His legs are covered to give protection when riding through vegetation, while the helmet gives added security.

BMX Racing

This branch of cycle racing is the one furthest removed from mainstream cycling, and is often regarded as a separate sport. A quick glance at the shape, size and equipment of a BMX bike will provide the explanation for this.

As with mountain bikes, BMX bikes originated in the United States and the enthusiasts there have evolved a language all their own. 'Wheelies', 'whoop-de-doos' and 'motos' are all terms unknown in traditional cycling.

Competition takes place on tracks laid out on areas of waste ground. A prerequisite is that the start point is higher than the finish: this enables the riders to get up speed to negotiate the various features of a typical course (see the following pages). In Britain, local authorities often provide the site and the materials necessary for its construction.

At a typical BMX race meeting, there are classifications for various age groups, from the under-eights to an open class for older teenagers and beyond. In each age group, a series of heats (or motos) are contested, with the best going through to a final at the end of the meeting. World championships are held annually for all age groups.

This system offers every starter a chance of some form of success – and this partly explains the sport's popularity with young people. As a rider proceeds from novice to expert, so the equipment becomes more sophisticated. Instead of steel, bike frames are manufactured from chrome-moly, a much lighter alloy. And much tougher chainsets,

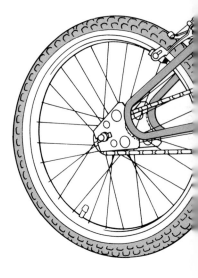

pedals, handlebars and wheels are necessary.

The bike has a single freewheel gear and definitely no toe-clips. The saddle is barely touched during a race as it is more effective to stand on the pedals and sprint. A race lasts 30 seconds.

To take part in BMX racing, a rider must wear long trousers and a motor cycle style crash-helmet. A long-sleeved top, thick gloves and sturdy training shoes are also favoured.

A moto normally has six starters, who line up behind a low gate that is flipped forward to start. As with BMX's big brother – motor cycle moto-cross – it is important to hit the front as soon as possible. The riders

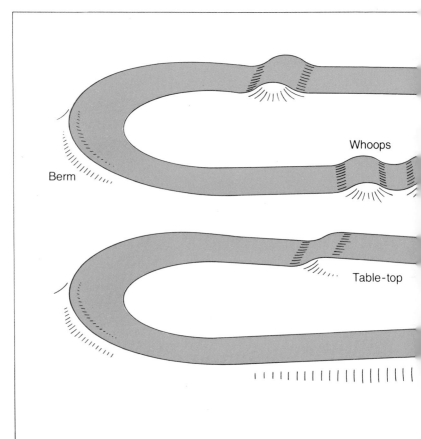

Berm

Whoops

Table-top

can then choose their own way through the tight, banked turns (or berms) and over the table-tops and whoop-de-doos.

The emphasis in BMX racing is on skill and technique rather than on physical strength, although the top-liners use normal road bikes to get themselves fitter than is possible on the BMX machines themselves.

A typical BMX race-track is laid out on waste-ground, with the various mounds and obstacles made up from compacted soil, gravel and rubble. The total length of the track will not exceed 438 yds (400 m). It takes much practice to perfect the various techniques, such as pre-jumping the whoops and table-tops, and pedalling through the banked turns.

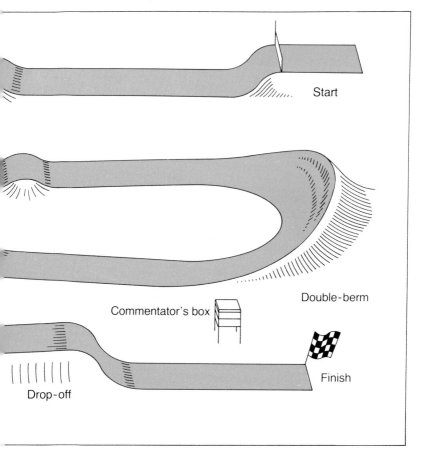

The Cycling Spectator

Since the sport's inception in the late nineteenth century, crowds have been an integral part of cycle racing – whether lining an Alpine pass on the route of the Tour de France, packing the infield of a smoke-filled arena at a German six-day race or massing in the streets of a British city at a televized circuit race. The riders respond to the enthusiasm of the crowds, and the resultant ambiance helps to make cycling a very visually attractive sport.

You may have seen some continental road racing or Olympic track racing on television and be interested in watching the sport live. Look for details of events in the cycling press (see **Newspapers and Magazines**, page 91). There may be a track race meeting or weekend road race in your area. If so, it could make a good destination for your Sunday ride. Check the starting-time and the full distance of road races; remember a 100-mile race will last about four hours, so an 11.00 a.m. start would mean a 3.00 p.m. finish. You would want to arrive about halfway through the race, particularly if the race is on, say, a circuit of ten miles, otherwise you could have a long wait.

The best place from which to watch a road race is near the top of a hill, where you can see the riders for longer. This is also the point where the most attacks are likely to begin. Plan to get to the finish area about half-an-hour before the end so that you can pick a good spot to watch the final sprints. You could ride your own bicycle home with dreams of becoming a racer yourself.

Understanding teamwork

It is often a mystery to the casual spectator why the apparently strongest rider in a race does not always win. What he or she does not understand is the strong element played by teamwork in any type of massed-start race. A typical example of a team at work in a road race is shown here. The situation is a wide, straight road with a strong wind blowing from the left. An echelon of riders forms at the front (above right) with three members of one team included in the line. The aim in a road race is to progressively increase the chances of winning. Obviously, to have three of a team in a breakaway group of perhaps 12 riders is better odds than a team of six in a field of 120: it is a 25 per cent chance instead of five. To make sure that the attack is restricted to only a few riders, the leaders race hard and keep to one side of the road (roads are closed to other traffic). An increase in pace causes the echelon to move clear with, typically, a single line of riders trying to join the front group. The hangers-on are forced by the wind to race in the gutter (right), unless a second echelon is formed. Seeing the situation, a team-mate of the three in front will deliberately leave a gap in the line of chasers (far right) to make sure that the task of jumping across the leaders is made more difficult, if not impossible. Ahead, the three team-mates will work hard with the others in the break to establish their advantage, and towards the end they will out-manoeuvre their opponents

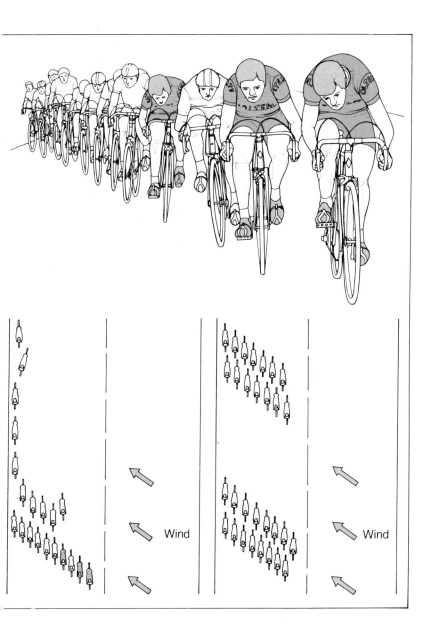

Wind

Wind

Exotic Equipment

In a century of cycling, the bicycle has changed little – it remains a diamond-shaped frame fitted with two (approximately) equal-sized wheels, a seat and handlebars, and powered by two pedals linked by a chain to a driving sprocket on the rear wheel. But, within that specification, technical developments have dragged this simple machine into the space age. In fact, many of the materials used in the most specialized racing bikes come directly from aerospace technology: titanium and magnesium alloys, and carbon fibre. Components and whole bikes are tested in wind tunnels to ensure maximum safety and efficiency.

Allied to the scientific research is the quest for more efficient and better-looking equipment. This is perhaps best illustrated by the evolution of the brake, an item that is rarely used in racing and then only to slow down. And yet, through the 1970s and 1980s, there has been great competition among rival manufacturers to produce the most exotic-looking brakes. The more expensive ones can cost ten times that of the traditional type. Instead of cables, nuts and bolts being exposed, the latest brakes are fully enclosed in a small triangular-shaped, streamlined housing. One cable emerges from the top, but it does not loop over the brake lever. Instead, it follows a path through the bicycle frame tube and handlebars to emerge tidily within the lever itself.

Front and rear derailleurs are similarly streamlined, with the jockey wheels and springs hidden beneath shiny alloy covers. Pedals have been reduced to tiny platforms onto which shoes may slot directly, perhaps without the use of toe-clips and straps. Chainwheels are cut away to weigh less, while crank arms are smoothed.

But perhaps the greatest advance has been in the wheels. At the top competitive levels, hubs and rims have acquired so-called low profile shapes which are narrower and smoother. Fewer spokes, with razor edges, enable the wheel to cut through the air.

Tyres are also narrower and sometimes inflated with helium, which is lighter than air. In trying to eliminate the drag caused by spokes (even the cut-throat variety), the so-called disc wheel was permitted in international competition for the first time at the 1984 Olympic Games and world championships.

Experiments have been made in the past with spoked wheels covered with a thin sheet of suitable material, but the present-day disc wheels are spokeless, gaining their strength from the discs themselves, which are made of carbon fibre or Kevlar. Some have a honeycomb construction, others are hollow, with lightweight packing to preserve the correct shape.

All these developments have helped to reduce the air drag caused by the bike; but it is the rider who still remains the biggest obstacle in aerodynamic terms. Teardrop-shaped helmets and covered shoes help, but little else can be done.

Streamlining/disc wheels

The illustration shows the type of bike and accessories that are used for the track pursuit race – a short-distance race against the clock where even thousandths of a second can mean the difference between winning and losing. The frame is made as low and thin as possible by using oval section tubing, and eliminating the high frontal area by angling the top tube down to the front forks. A smaller front wheel has helped this development.

Instead of the normal 28 or 36 spokes, this front wheel has only 14, with the spoke edges filed to razor thinness. The wheel rims are triangular in section and perhaps half the width of a rim you would see on a normal road bike. The thin tyres will be inflated with helium for lightness.

The rear wheel does not have any spokes: it comprises two carbon discs that are joined to a specially narrow hub and low profile rim. The discs eliminate the constant eddy currents that are created by spokes. But you cannot eliminate the drag forces caused by the rider's moving legs!

Part 3 Care and Maintenance

Mending a puncture

1 Whether you are going to mend the puncture or simply change the inner tube, the first task is to remove the wheel. If the hub does not have quick-release mechanisms, you will need the correct sized spanner to loosen the track nuts (as shown). If you have to remove the rear wheel, it is better to prop the bicycle upside-down, on saddle and handlebars. If you have a freewheel block, change the derailleur into top gear. It makes removal easier.

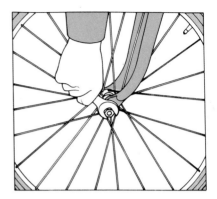

2 For wired-on tyres, you will need three tyre-levers to force one side of the tyre over the edge of the rim. The nut on the air valve has to be removed, then place the spoon-shaped end of the first two tyre-levers between the rim and the tyre from above. Putting pressure on the free end of the lever will loosen the tyre edge; if it is stubborn, using two levers close together may do the trick. The notch in the lever end is to hook around a spoke while working another lever.

3 Avoid pinching the inner tube while using the tyre-levers, and then carefully remove the tube by hand. Connect the pump to the valve and slightly inflate the inner tube. It is sometimes obvious where it is punctured; if not, partly fill a bowl or bucket (or use a convenient pond or stream!) and as shown, immerse the tube in the water. A bubble, or bubbles, will come from the puncture. Put your finger on it and then mark it with a wax crayon.

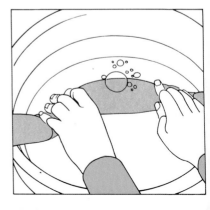

4 With the puncture located and marked, dry the area of tube around the hole before applying a thin coating of the solution. Select a patch that will adequately cover the hole(s). When the adhesive has dried on the tube, strip off the covering to the patch and place firmly over the hole (see right). Working from the centre, gradually apply pressure to make sure that no air is trapped under the patch.

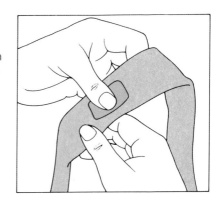

5 Before replacing the tube in the tyre, partly inflate the tube to make sure that the puncture is indeed mended. To replace the tube, first push the valve back through its hole in the rim and screw on the retainer nut. Then gently push the inner tube back into the tyre cover, making sure that it does not become twisted. You can now push the tyre back into the rim, starting beside the valve. It is not necessary to use tyre-levers.

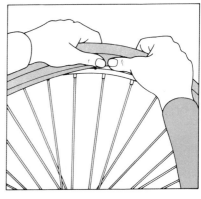

6 With the tyre back on the rim, check that the inner tube has not been pinched. If it has, carefully push it back into position before fully inflating the tyre. Before refitting the wheel, make sure that the brake quick-release is still open, otherwise you could easily knock one of the brake blocks from its housings. When the wheel is back in the forks, hold it in its correct, centred position before re-tightening the nuts.

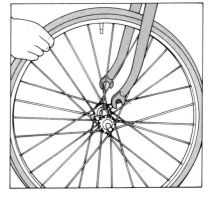

Maintenance of Brakes

Replacing brake blocks

Do not wait until the brake blocks are worn down beyond the pattern of studs. Make sure you get new ones that are the correct model and length for your brakes. There are different types for centre-pull models (see right) and side-pull ones (see below). Before removing the blocks, make sure you know in which direction they are pointing so that you can refit them correctly. You will notice that the blocks slot into a housing that has three raised edges; the open end, into which the block is pushed, always points backwards, the raised end forwards. Always check with the dealer that the new blocks are compatible with the rims on your bike – alloy and steel rims require different types of block. When making final adjustments, always ensure that the two blocks line up with the rim edge.

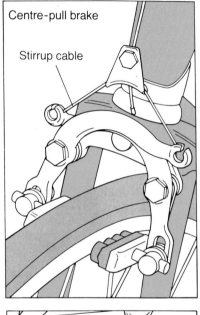

Centre-pull brake

Stirrup cable

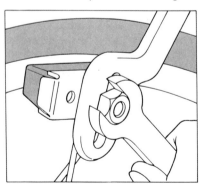

1 The blocks are fixed to the brake arms by dome-headed nuts which also set the position of the brake shoes relative to the rim. If the nut is too tight for a small spanner, it may be necessary to use a long-handled adjustable spanner to remove it.

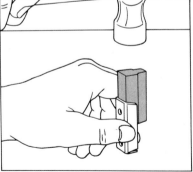

2 Removing the blocks from the shoes sometimes needs a little coaxing with a pair of pliers or a screwdriver, while fitting the new ones could demand the (gentle) use of a hammer to tap them in. Clean the brake shoes before refitting the blocks

Replacing the brake cables

When a brake cable becomes frayed or kinked at the end, it is time to replace it. You will need to loosen the nut and pull the cable out from the brake lever end. It is often advisable to replace the outer cable as well if this has become kinked. Ready-lubricated cables and covers can be bought, and will give more efficient service than a separate cable which needs to be greased before insertion. When the cable is refitted and adjusted, a plastic cap can be placed on the end (see right). Make sure the nut is fully tightened.

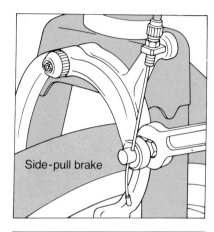

Side-pull brake

Adjusting brakes

After the replacement of brake blocks or a cable, the brake needs adjustment. You need to hold the brake arms together while the cable is pulled through with a pair of pliers and the fixing nut is tightened. (There is a tool appropriately named 'the third hand' on the market, otherwise get a friend to help.) When the rough adjustment has been made, the brake blocks can be brought closer to (or further from) the rim by turning the barrel adjuster. The method is different for centre-pull brakes which do not need to be pulled together and tightened at the same time. The short cable linking the two brake arms is first disconnected by pinching the brake shoes together. The actual adjustment is done on the main cable by releasing the nut that fixes the small metal stirrup. Make sure that you do not twist the cable when retightening this nut. Again, fine tuning can be carried out with the barrel adjuster.

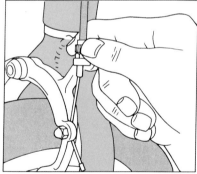

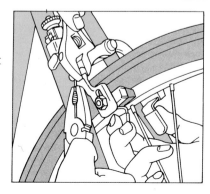

Maintenance of Transmission

Derailleur gears

A derailleur gear can need adjustment for a number of reasons: a stretched cable, a damaged (bent) gear arm or a change of block (say, from five sprockets, as shown, to six or seven). Most derailleurs work on the principle whereby the inner cable is untensioned when the chain is on the outside (small) sprocket; therefore the cable can be pulled through and tightened when the gear is in this position. Ensure that the gear lever adjustment bolt is fully tightened (it could be hand-adjusted or require a screwdriver). To adjust the lateral throw of the gear itself, there are two separate, tensioned screws – one stops the chain being pulled beyond the outer sprocket, the other stops it going into the spokes. This is a simple adjustment with a screwdriver. The front derailleur should be similarly adjusted. The bicycle can be stood upside-down so you can turn the pedals. The two small jockey wheels need occasional lubrication and the cables should be replaced when there are kinks or signs of fraying.

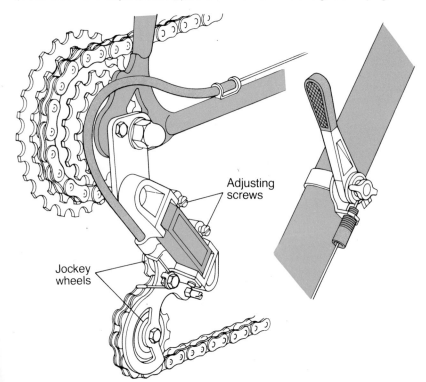

Adjusting screws

Jockey wheels

Hub gears

Although the mechanism of a hub gear is fully enclosed, it requires regular lubrication with a light oil. The different makes and models need different alignment to be correctly adjusted, but the normal three-speed Sturmey-Archer gear is adjusted as follows. First put the gear lever (trigger) in second gear, then loosen the cable lock-nut and hold the cable connection as shown. This should be screwed up or down until the hub axle is in line with the indicator rod (as seen through the 'window').

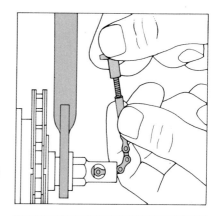

Chains and pedals

There are more moving parts in a chain than in the rest of the bike, and it is the item on which there is the most pressure. Consequently, you should make regular checks for signs of wear: tight links, bent side-plates or excessive stretching. The chain also causes wear in sprocket and chainwheel teeth. For a single or hub gear, the chain tension can be checked, as shown, with a small screwdriver: there should be about ½ in (12 mm) play, up and down. This can be adjusted by moving the rear wheel slightly forwards or backwards after loosening the hub. If there is a build-up of dirt and/or grease on the chain, it can be cleaned, as shown, with an old tooth-brush, but a more thorough job can be done by removing the chain (prise off the spring link for single and hub gears, or remove two rivets with a link extractor tool for derailleur chains) and soaking it in a tray of paraffin. Dry the chain carefully and re-lubricate it after cleaning.

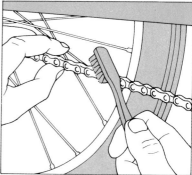

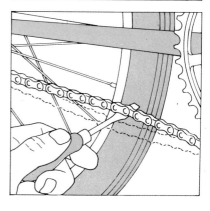

Maintenance of Accessories

The saddle

The majority of saddles made today are formed from plastic, perhaps with a padded and thin leather (or suede) covering. Such seats should not deform, and require little maintenance other than cleaning with a damp cloth or, in the case of suede, brushing with a plastic or rubber bristled brush. When wet, leather saddles need to be dried slowly, with the application of two or three coats of a preservative such as Proofide. If the leather sags after much use, the bolt (right) should be tightened slightly. If this is overdone, the saddle will become deformed.

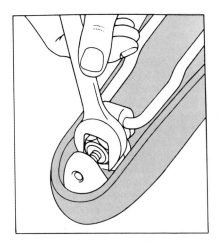

Handlebars

When the tape on your handlebars gets discoloured, cut or plain grubby, it is time to replace it. This usually entails removing the handlebar end plug and then unravelling the tape, which can be either sticky or non-adhesive plastic. It will probably be necessary to loosen the brake levers – you may also wish to adjust their position before re-taping. Most riders prefer to leave about 2 ins (5 cm) of metal each side of the stem, but if you use the bike in cold weather, it is advisable to start taping next to the stem (see right). Tape the bars slowly, making sure that each turn gives an overlap of about ⅛ in. (3 mm). At the brake lever, roll back the rubber hood and slightly loosen the lever so that it can be taped over the clip but under the hood. About 3 ins (8 cm) can be left to poke into the handlebar end before the end plug is inserted. Padded sleeves are an alternative covering.

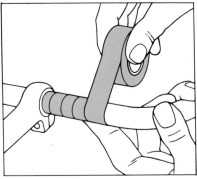

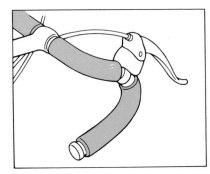

Lights

Little actual maintenance is required
on lighting equipment, but whether
the choice is dynamo-driven or
battery lamps, regular checks must
be made. There are three types of
dynamo: those driven off the rear tyre
tread, off the front or rear side-wall
(both illustrated) or by the hub (in a
unit combining a hub gear). With all
three systems, it is important that the
electrical contacts are kept clean,
and that you always have with you
spare bulbs of the right voltage
should one fail during a ride. Also, the
generator should be lubricated as
recommended by the manufacturer, if
at all. Obviously, both dynamo and
battery lamps should have their front
and rear faces cleaned before each
use. Traditional dry cell and
rechargeable batteries must be
checked regulary for power output.
When the light beam has started to
drop in intensity, the batteries should
be replaced (or recharged). *Never*
leave batteries in the lamp for long
periods when the bike is not in use;
batteries can 'leak' and corrode the
lamp terminals, making it inoperable.
The two battery lamps shown here
slot into plastic holders, but the
heavier variety of lamp can often work
loose on a standard bracket; it is
advisable to prevent this by using a
stout rubber-band or strap to keep
the lamp on tightly. Before buying
new lamps, check with the dealer that
they have the correct specification;
Great Britain and some American
states have strict laws on what type
and size of lights should be used.
Similarly, your bike should also have
reflectors.

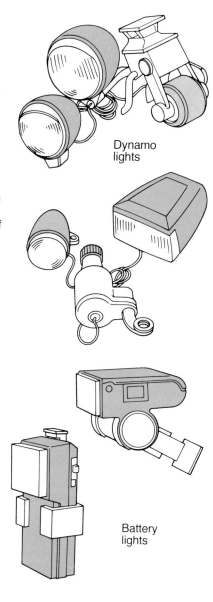

Dynamo
lights

Battery
lights

Transporting Bikes

Up to four bikes can be carried on a roof-rack such as this, on which the bike is fixed by a quick-release front hub mechanism and a strap around the rear rim.

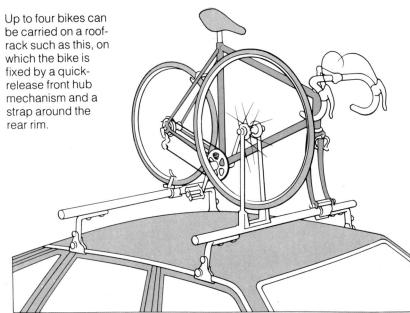

By car

Whether you wish to travel by car to a race, to go touring in a new area or to drive to within cycle commuting distance of work, you will need some form of bicycle rack, unless the car boot will easily accommodate the bike, with its wheels removed. If you already have a normal roof-rack, you can strap the bike on upside-down (make sure the saddle is covered and padded). Toe-straps are best for holding on the bike at the saddle and at either side of the handlebars. Whether using a traditional rack, or one of the specific bike-carrying types shown here, make doubly sure before each trip that both the bicycle and the rack are bolted down or tied on to the car roof securely.

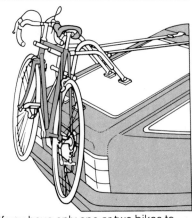

If you have only one or two bikes to transport, this boot-rack can be sufficient. The complete machine is supported by two protruding rods. Car wing-mirrors are essential.

The folding bike

The sole reason for buying a folding bike is that its transportation is a priority. Most of these machines are supplied with a carrying-bag, which can be used when taking the bike on a train, coach or plane. If you travel a lot by car, it is convenient to keep a folding bike permanently in the boot, so that you can use it whenever you feel like a ride or wish to travel the last leg of a commuting trip into a city centre. Check the size the bike folds to against the size of your car-boot before buying!

Right: It should take less than a minute to put a folding bike into its compact shape as shown here. It is more convenient and secure to carry a bike in a boot than on a rack.

Airline bags

Transporting a bike by air should not be a problem, especially with a custom-made bag. In the boxes supplied by some airlines it is necessary to remove the wheels from the bike, and probably reverse the pedals in the cranks so that they point inwards. A touring bike will usually need to have its mudguards removed and perhaps the racks. If you travel regularly by air, then a bag like this will provide good protection in transit, and will be convenient for carrying when you arrive. Remember to take tools for the bike's reassembly.

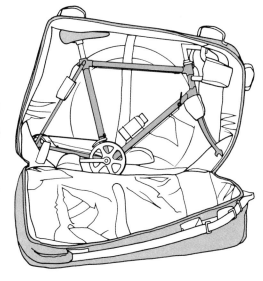

Records

World records in cycling do not have the same importance in the sport as they do, for instance, in athletics. This is because a track cycling record cannot be set in actual competition; the rider has to be alone on the track, racing against time.

The most important record is the World Hour Record, in which the rider has to ride alone on a velodrome and race as far as he can in 60 minutes. This record was established in 1893 by the Frenchman Henri Desgrange (who also started the Tour de France ten years later), when he rode 35.325 km on the Buffalo track in Paris.

Only 18 cyclists have since managed to improve on this achievement with the record being held in 1985 by Francesco Moser of Italy, who completed 51.151 km on the Mexico City Sports Centre track. Moser rode a revolutionary bicycle that utilized disc wheels for the first time. During his two successful attempts on the hour record, Moser broke three other professional world records: 5 km in 5 minutes 47.16 seconds, 10 km in 11:39.75 and 20 km in 23:21.59.

There are separate world records for amateurs, professionals and women and, in each category, for outdoor and indoor velodromes. At the shorter distances – 200 metres, 500 metres and one km – there are also separate records for standing starts and flying starts.

For road racing, records are recognized for the fastest average speed of the winner. There can be no direct comparison between races on different courses, but a so-called 'Yellow Ribbon' is awarded for the fastest classic race longer than 225 km. The holder since 1975 has been Freddy Maertens of Belgium who won that year's Paris to Brussels race, 285.5 km, at an average speed of 46.110 km per hr. The actual fastest long-distance road race was the Milan to Vignola event in Italy in 1981, when Gregor Braun of West Germany completed the 216 km at a speed of 47.801 km per hr. As for the world's most famous race, the Tour de France, the record speed was set in 1981 by Bernard Hinault of France who completed the 3,756.6 km at an average speed of 37.987 km per hr.

In Great Britain, there is an established system of records set in time trials (known as competition records) over the set lengths of 10, 25, 50 and 100 miles, and 12 and 24 hours. These records are constantly being broken due to the improving quality of bikes and road surfaces, and the increased use of dual carriageways (with consequent assistance from traffic flow). For the shorter distances, average speeds of more than 30 mph (about 50 km/hr) have been recorded, while more than 500 miles (800 km) have been completed in 24-hour time trials, an average speed of more than 21 mph (34 km/hr).

There also exists a large number of road records, in which a rider has to perform completely alone. Many of these are place-to-place routes, such as the longest, Land's End to John O'Groats – approximately 840 miles (1350 km) – for which the record is less than two days.

Similar records exist in places such as Australia and America, with the longest regularly contested route being coast-to-coast in the United States, a distance of 3,000 miles. Several riders have completed this in less than ten days.

Races

A complex schedule of international racing has evolved in the one hundred years since road racing first grew into a major sport in continental Europe. There are amateur races, professional races and so-called open races (in which amateurs can race against professionals under strictly enforced rules).

Those races that carry the most prestige are for professionals. In a typical season in Europe, the calendar comprises five distinct phases:

1 Early season stage races, such as the Mediterranean Tour and Paris–Nice in France; the Tour of Sardinia and Tirreno–Adriatico in Italy; and the Ruta del Sol and Valencia Tour in Spain.

2 The spring classics (long distance, one-day races), including Milan–San Remo (Italy); the Tour of Flanders and Liège–Bastogne–Liège (Belgium); and Paris–Roubaix (France).

3 The stage races and 'Tours' that include the three-week-long Tour de France, Tour of Italy and Tour of Spain; the ten-day Tour of Switzerland; and the one-week, or shorter, Tour of Luxembourg, Tour de Romandie (in Switzerland),

Dauphiné–Libéré (in France), the Tour of Belgium, and the Tour of the Basque Country (in Spain).

4 The so-called criteriums, which are short-distance (usually less than 100 km) races on small, closed circuits (less than 2 km around), that are held in small towns and villages. The stars of the big classics and tours are paid start-money for these races, which take place from the end of July to the end of August prior to the major one-day race of the professional season, the 260 km World Road Race Championship.

5 The autumn classics, a series of one-day races similar to those held in springtime, including Paris–Brussels, Blois–Chaville (in France) and the Tour of Lombardy (Italy).

Certain of these professional races are 'open' but only to amateurs of more than 25 years of age. This is because amateurs are restricted to a maximum one-day distance of 200 km and an average of around 150 km.

The principal amateur races are national and intra-national stage races, such as the Peace Race (in eastern Europe), usually between the cities of Warsaw, Berlin and Prague), the Milk Race (or Tour of Britain), the Coors Classic (or Tour of Colorado, USA), the Tour de l'Avenir (a mini Tour de France) and the Brisbane–Sydney (Australia).

The main single-day races are at the annual world championships and the Olympic Games, where the three medal events are the 200 km road race for men, the 80 km road race for women and the 100 km team time trial.

Organizations

UK and Eire
Audax UK, 188 Runcorn Road, Warrington, Cheshire WA4 6SY. Controls and organizes tourist-type *randonneur* rides in Great Britain.

British Cycling Federation (BCF), 16 Upper Woburn Place, London WC1H 0QE. The governing body for all forms of cycle racing in Great Britain.

British Cyclo-Cross Association, 8 Bellam Road, Hampton Magna, near Warwick. Controls cyclo-cross racing in Great Britain.

Cyclists' Touring Club (CTC), Cotterell House, 69 Meadrow, Godalming, Surrey GU7 3HS. Provides information, free insurance, newsletter and defence of cyclists' rights for members, mostly cycle tourists.

English Schools Cycling Association, 6 Malmerswell Road, High Wycombe, Bucks. Organizes cycling for schools, with annual championships.

Irish Cycling Federation, 287 Castletown, Leixlip, Co. Kildare. Internationally recognized governing body for cycling in the Irish Republic.

National BMX Association, 13 Chelford Avenue, Lowton, Warrington, Cheshire.

National Cycling Association, 24 The Gables, Kill, Co. Kildare. Alternative cycle racing organization to the Irish Cycling Federation in the Irish Republic.

Northern Ireland Cycling Federation, 2A Upper Malone Road, Belfast. Controls racing in Ulster as part of the Irish Cycling Tripartite Committee.

Professional Cycling Association, 30 Windermere Road, Wolverhampton WV6 9DL. Controls professional racing in Great Britain.

Road Time Trials Council, Dallacre, Mill Road, Yarwell, Peterborough PE8 6PS. Controls road time trial competition in England and Wales.

RoSPA (the Royal Society for the Prevention of Accidents), Cannon House, Priory Queensway, Birmingham 4. Organizes the national cycling proficiency scheme and runs the National Bike Club, an organization for all cyclists who are not members of the BCF or CTC.

The Tandem Club, 25 Hendred Way, Abingdon, Oxon OX14 2AN. Provides information for all tandem riders.

UKBMX, 5 Church Hill, Staplehurst, Tonbridge, Kent. Governing body for cyclo-cross racing in Great Britain.

Women's Cycle Racing Association, 44 Melin Road, Romford, Essex RM5 3YH. Organizes championship races for women.

North America
Bicycle USA, PO Box 988, 19 East Read Street, Baltimore, MD 21203. Formerly the League of American Wheelmen, this is the US equivalent of the Cyclists' Touring Club.

Bikecentennial, PO Box 8308, Missoula, MA 59807. Provides touring information.

Canadian Cycling Association, 333 River Road, Vanier, Ottawa K1L 8B9, Ontario. Governing body for all forms of cycle racing in Canada.

United States Cycling Federation, 1750 East Boulder Street, Colorado Springs, CO 80909. Governing body for all forms of cycle racing.

Newspapers and Magazines

In Great Britain, the sport of cycle racing is reported most extensively in the three 'quality' daily newspapers, the *Daily Telegraph*, the *Guardian* and *The Times*. The *Daily Express* and *Daily Mail* also have specific cycling correspondents. In Ireland, the *Irish Independent, Irish Press* and the *Irish Times* all give prominent coverage of cycling. In the magazine field, the only weekly publication is *Cycling*, which comprehensively reports the home and overseas racing scene, as well as on leisure cycling and touring.

Of the many monthly magazines, the glossiest is *Winning: Bicycle Racing Illustrated*, which has 100 pages, all in colour, devoted to the sport on an international scale. In the category of part racing/part touring/part technical magazines, *Bicycle Action* is more broadly based than *Bicycle Magazine, Bicycle Times* and *Cycling World*. *Cycletouring* is the journal of the Cyclists Touring Club available free to members. For BMX fans, *BMX Action Bike* is the glossiest, followed by *BMX Bi-Weekly*.

In Ireland, the *Irish Cycling Review* is the only specialist publication.

Other English language magazines published around the world include *Australian Cycling* and *National Cycling* for Australia and New Zealand and a wide selection in the United States. Of the American publications, the most widely read is *Bicycling*, that concentrates on the scientific testing of bicycles, components and touring. Its main rival in this field is *Bicycle Guide*, while the equally colourful *Cyclist* includes racing features. The principal sports magazine is the US edition of *Winning: Bicycle Racing Illustrated*, which includes the European features, plus extensive coverage of American events.

Most European countries produce their own cycling publications. In France, *Miroir du Cyclisme, Vélo* and *Sprint International* cater for the racing market, and *Le Cycle* for the tourist and technical market. The Netherlands has *Wieler Revue* and *Fiets*, West Germany *Radsport* and *Tour*, and Italy *Bicisport* and *Bicicletta*.

British Publications

Bicycle Action, 134 Tooley Street, London SE1 (01-403 6655).

Bicycle Magazine, 89–91 Bayham Street, Camden Town, London NW1 0AG (01-482 2040).

Bicycle Times, 26 Commercial Buildings, Dunston, Tyne & Wear. NE11 9AA (0632 608113).

Cycletouring, Cotterell House, 69 Meadrow, Godalming, Surrey GU7 3HS (04868 7217).

Cycling, Surrey House, 1 Throwley Way, Sutton, Surrey SM1 4QQ (01-643 8040).

Cycling World, Andrew House, 2A Granville Road, Sidcup, Kent DA14 4BN.

Winning: Bicycle Racing Illustrated, 120 St. Margaret's Road, Twickenham, Middlesex TW1 2AA. (01-891 4931).

BMX Action Bike, 134 Tooley Street, London SE1 (01-403 6655).

BMX Bi-Weekly, Market Street, Morecambe, Lancs (0524 422897).

Bibliography

General and Maintenance

The Penguin Bicycle Handbook by Rob van der Plas (Penguin, 1983). Illustrated technical paperback covering bicycle frames, gearing, maintenance and allied subjects.

Richard's Bicycle Book by Richard Ballantine (Pan, 1975, updated 1983). Idiosyncratic paperback on the whys and why-nots of bicycle riding and maintenance.

The New Cyclist by Tony Osman (Collins, 1982). Large format paperback, covering in an easy style the history of the bicycle, maintenance, the touring and pleasure cyclist, and cycling for health.

Bicycle: the Total Illustrated Guide to Bicycles and Bicycling by John Wilcockson (Marshall Cavendish, 1980). Lavishly illustrated hardback, covering everything from bicycle history, through cycling proficiency and maintenance, to the technical aspects of touring and racing.

Cycle Touring

Cycling in Europe by Nicholas Crane (Pan, 1985). Entertaining and practical paperback guide to touring (and enjoying the experience) in 16 countries of continental Europe.

The CTC Book of Cycling by John Whatmore (David & Charles, 1983). A sparsely illustrated hardback, which is half a general introduction to bicycle and touring, half a detailed gazetteer to touring routes in Britain.

Weekend Cycling by Christa Gausden (Oxford Illustrated Press, 1981). Exhaustive guide to suitable weekend touring routes at centres throughout Great Britain.

The CTC Route Guide to Cycling in Britain and Ireland by Nicholas Crane & Christa Gausden (Pan, 1981). Detailed paperback on interconnecting touring routes throughout the British Isles.

Adventure Cycling in Britain by Tim Hughes (1978). Comprehensive guide to the many technical aspects of touring, with useful map section.

Cycle Racing

The Fabulous World of Cycling: Season 1984 by Léon Michaux and Eddy Merckx (Winning Productions, 1985). Lavish colour photography and informed comment of the 1984 racing season in Europe and the United States, with the Olympic Games highlights. (This is an annual publication.)

Agonistic Cycling by Agostino Massogrande (Edizione Londoni, 1983). A translation of an Italian handbook on race training.

The Complete Cycle Sport Guide by Peter Konopka (EP, 1982). Complete manual on training for cycle racing, translated from German.

Barry Hoban: Watching the Wheels Go Round, an autobiography with John Wilcockson (Stanley Paul, 1981). The fascinating life story of Barry Hoban, the Englishman who won eight stages of the Tour de France in a lengthy professional career.

Tour de France: the 75th Anniversary Cycle Race by Robin Magowan (1979). A cerebral account of the 1978 Tour de France, with a good section on the history of the world's most famous bike race.

The Great Bike Race by Geoffrey

Nicholson (Magnum, 1977). A highly descriptive account of the 1976 Tour de France, with details of the race's intriguing elements.

Cycle Racing: Training to Win by Les Woodland (Pelham, 1975). Basic manual on the different aspects of training and racing for beginners.

Cycling-related Books

International Cycling Guide edited by Nicholas Crane (Tantivy Press, 1984). Annual edition that covers the complete world of cycling, with exhaustive section on latest technical developments.

The Puffin BMX Handbook by Richard Grant (Puffin, 1984). A clear, concise guide to the world of BMX racing.

Merlyn the Magician and the Pacific Coast Highway by Tom Davies (New English Library, 1983). A fascinating travelogue, both amusing and emotional, by a writer who takes his bike with him on various international assignments.

Journey to the Source of the Nile by Nick Sanders (NMS, 1983). A travel book, colourfully illustrated and colourfully written, on this cycling explorer's African expedition.

Ride it! BMX by Don Smith (Haynes, 1982). A basic hardback introduction to BMX riding and racing.

Cycling by Jeanne Mackenzie (Oxford University Press, 1981). An anthology of the bicycle as written in poetry and literature.

The Penguin Book of the Bicycle by Roderick Watson & Martin Gray (Penguin, 1978). A well-illustrated paperback that takes a modern view of the world of cycling in all its forms.

Cycling: Fitness on Wheels by John Wilcockson (World's Work/The Sunday Times, 1978). An inspirational guide to improving physical fitness by cycling.

Index